Tunes & Wooden Spoons

Come In, the Kettle's On!

Mary Janet MacDonald & Margie MacDonald

MacIntyre Purcell Publishing Inc.

MacIntyre Purcell Publishing Inc.
232 Fairmont Road
Cloverville, Nova Scotia
B2G 2K9

(902) 640-3350

www.macintyrepurcell.com
info@macintyrepurcell.com

Cover and book design: Gwen North

ISBN: 978-1-77276-195-5

Printed and bound in Canada by Friesens

Library and Archives Canada Cataloguing in Publication

Title: Tunes and wooden spoons : come in, the kettle's on! / Mary Janet MacDonald & Margie MacDonald.
Other titles: Come in, the kettle's on!
Names: MacDonald, Mary Janet, author | MacDonald, Margie (Author), author.
Identifiers: Canadiana 20250199858 | ISBN 9781772761955 (softcover)
Subjects: LCSH: Baking—Maritime Provinces. | LCSH: Cooking, Canadian—Maritime Provinces style. | LCGFT: Cookbooks.
Classification: LCC TX765 .M3182 2025 | DDC 641.81/5—dc23

MacIntyre Purcell Publishing Inc. would like to acknowledge the financial support of the Government of Canada and the Nova Scotia Department of Tourism, Culture and Heritage.

Canada Council for the Arts Conseil des Arts du Canada

As an organization operating in Cloverville, Nova Scotia, we acknowledge that the land on which we conduct our business is the traditional and unceded territory of the Mi'kmaq People. We pay our respects to the Elders, past and present, and express our gratitude for their stewardship of this land throughout the generations. We recognize Indigenous peoples' ongoing presence and contributions to our community and commit to fostering meaningful relationships based on mutual respect, understanding, and collaboration.

TABLE OF CONTENTS

This book is dedicated to my grandmothers Jessie Isabel Margaret Beaton (February 17, 1887–January 11, 1951) and Mary Catherine (Cassie) Cameron (May 3, 1892–March 18, 1953).

Jessie Belle and I share the same birthday, a connection I've always cherished. She married my grandfather Alexander MacDonald on September 24, 1912, in Mabou, Cape Breton Island, Nova Scotia. Together, they had four children: Flora Mae, Catherine Ann, John Donald, and Donald — my father.

Mary Cassie married my grandfather John Andrew MacDonell on November 23, 1913, also in Mabou, Cape Breton Island. They raised an incredible family of 17 children, including my mother, Margaret Ann.

Looking at wedding photos from my grandmothers' era, I noticed how solemn the couples appeared — no smiles, just serious expressions. Unfortunately, I couldn't find high-quality pictures of either grandmother to truly capture them. Wanting to bring them to life in a new way, I turned to Terry MacDonald, an artist in Inverness, Cape Breton. I asked him to take a little artistic liberty — to give these remarkable women a smile. He did just that, and I absolutely love the result. Somehow, in that small change, they feel more alive than ever before.

So here's to Jessie Belle and Mary Cassie. Though I never had the chance to know you, I carry you with me always. Through you, I had the gift of life, and through this book, I celebrate your legacy. I love you both.

INTRODUCTION

What a pleasure it is to share the one hundred plus cherished recipes in this cookbook! *Come In, the Kettle's On* completes a trilogy, following *Recipes from a Cape Breton Kitchen* and *Love Without Measure*, the first two books from the *Tunes and Wooden Spoons* series.

This collection is especially meaningful, as 41 of these recipes come from 39 grandmothers and two grandfathers, with the rest gathered from my own kitchen, from family and friends — recipes that have been lovingly passed down and shared over time. True to tradition, many recipes bear the names of those who shared them, like Peggy's Coconut Squares or Catherine Ann's Apple Muffins or Lottie's Orange Cake, keeping their memory alive with every bite.

What made this journey even more special was once again sharing the writing journey with my daughter Margie. Beyond her teaching career, Margie has a deep passion for photography, and together, we travelled across the Maritimes, visiting incredible home cooks and bakers, with her capturing the essence of each and every person we had the pleasure of visiting.

One thing stood out above all else — the joy of visiting. Let's bring back visiting! Take the time to drop in on a friend or relative, share a cup of tea or coffee, and bring along something homemade. No need to call first — just surprise them. The warmth we experienced in every home, the open doors and the heartfelt hospitality, left an imprint on our hearts. We arrived as guests and left as old friends.

I hope you'll embrace this book, cherish the stories and recipes within, and take inspiration to bake, share, and reconnect with those around you. There's something truly special about gathering over good food.

And if you ever find yourself in Port Hood, Nova Scotia — come in, the kettle's on!

A NOTE ABOUT THE NOMINATION PROCESS

Margie and I set out to create a Maritime cookbook, with a promise to personally visit each of the selected grandmothers. We opened a one-month nomination period, inviting grandchildren (or their designates) to tell us why their grandmother should be featured.

Over 150 heartfelt nominations poured in — each province represented, though we didn't know the exact communities. We ultimately chose 39 grandmothers, and their nominators had the joy of delivering the news before we arranged visits over the next five months.

When I first shared the project on my *Tunes and Wooden Spoons Facebook* page, one comment stood out: "What about grandfathers?" I reached out, and though he'd been joking, he eventually agreed to be included. I knew one other grandfather —an early supporter from Halifax — and with his family's help, he joined the lineup too. In the end, 39 grandmothers and two grandfathers welcomed us into their kitchens, and every visit was unforgettable.

So folks – it's all about the love – love for the grandchildren, love for the grandparents, love in the goodies, love in the kitchen, and especially love in the sunsets. Thank you one and all.

Confederation Bridge between New Brunswick and Prince Edward Island.

At the big fiddle in Sydney, Cape Breton.

Reading nominations en route to Halifax.

COOKIES AND SQUARES

Featured Grandmother

Minnie van de Wiel

"She is quick to share recipes and offer tips but is also still very keen and curious about learning from others too."

OMA'S SOFT MOLASSES CRINKLES

Minnie van de Wiel's recipe

INGREDIENTS

½ cup butter (room temperature)
½ cup margarine (room temperature)
2 cups packed brown sugar
2 eggs
½ cup molasses
4 ½ cups flour
2 teaspoons salt
4 teaspoons baking soda
2 teaspoons ginger
1 teaspoon cloves
2 teaspoons cinnamon

METHOD

Cream the butter and margarine and whip with electric beater. Add the brown sugar and continue to beat – scraping the sides of the bowl. Beat in the eggs, and then the molasses.

Measure out the flour in a separate bowl and then scoop out almost a cup of the flour into another bowl and add in the salt, soda, cloves, cinnamon, and ginger. Mix and add to the butter mixture and beat with electric beater. Add the rest of the flour a cup at a time, beating after each addition and then switch to a wooden spoon for the last cup.

Use a 2-tablespoon scoop or roll into balls and dip in some white sugar and place on a parchment-lined cookie sheet.

Bake at 360°F for 14 minutes.

Minnie met us at the door with a warm smile and led us straight into her immaculate kitchen located in her house on the Lower South River, Nova Scotia. It was impossible not to be impressed by her perfectly organized baking cupboard — every ingredient in its place, ready for the next batch of cookies or loaf of bread.

Minnie has always been busy. As a mother, she poured her energy into raising her children, and now she devotes just as much love and attention to baking with her many grandchildren.

They say the apple doesn't fall far from the tree, and in Minnie's case, that applies to her baking as well. According to one of her children, her cookies are just like her mother's — right down to the subtle, batch-to-batch variations. They are always perfect and, more importantly, perfectly familiar. Baking with her grandkids is one of her greatest joys, a way to pass down not just recipes but memories, laughter, and tradition.

Minnie is at her happiest when sharing — whether it's cookies, recipes, or baking tips. She is always generous with her knowledge but remains just as eager to learn from others, proving that even the most skilled bakers never stop growing. Her kitchen is a place of warmth, wisdom, and wonder, where every bite of a cookie holds a story, and every shared moment is a treasured gift.

Minnie's advice to her grandchildren: *"You are all a special gift for me. If you make a mistake, learn and move on. I am very proud to call you my grandkids. Remember, I will always love you to infinity and beyond. God Bless."*

ICE BOX GINGER COOKIES

It was a pleasure to have PEI's songstress, Patricia Murray, along with Carol, her mother, on my Tunes and Wooden Spoons *show and to include their versatile cookie recipe in this book. Make the dough, freeze the dough, and then slice off as many cookies as you want when you need them. So good with a cup of tea.*

INGREDIENTS

Large Bowl:

1 cup butter (room temperature)
1 cup brown sugar
2/3 cup molasses

Small Bowl:

Sift the following together:
2 3/4 cups all-purpose flour
2 teaspoons baking soda
2 teaspoons ginger
1/2 teaspoon cloves
1/2 teaspoon cinnamon
1/2 teaspoon salt

METHOD

Cream butter and mix with sugar until combined. Stir in the molasses until incorporated. Set aside.

Whisk dry ingredients together and add to butter mixture. Mix well.

Split the dough into 2 or 3 rectangular logs about 3 1/2 inches in width and about 1 1/2 inches high. Cover each log with wax paper or plastic wrap.

Refrigerate overnight or at least for 2–3 hours or put in freezer until you want to bake them.

Baking:

Preheat oven to 350°F. Prepare cookie sheet with parchment paper and take one log out of fridge (or freezer) and slice off 12 or more cookies (thinly sliced – approximately 1/8 inch). Space well as they spread. Bake around 7–9 minutes, but watch carefully after the 7-minute mark.

When taken out of the oven, leave the cookies on the pan on the cooling rack until the cookies are set. They should be hard and crisp. So good with a cup of tea! Best to store these in a cookie tin or a glass cookie jar to keep the crispness. If stored in plastic container, they tend to soften and are still good but won't have that good "snap".

MAPLE PECAN COOKIES

A recipe from Dave Kennedy, a friend of our son Mitchell.

INGREDIENTS

Bowl 1:

2 ⅓ cups flour
1 teaspoon baking soda
½ teaspoon salt

Bowl 2:

1 cup dark brown sugar (or regular yellow brown sugar)
½ cup soft butter
1 egg
⅓ cup maple syrup
1 teaspoon vanilla
1 teaspoon maple flavouring
½ cup chopped pecans (optional)

METHOD

Whisk the ingredients in bowl 1 and set aside.

Mix the sugar, butter, and egg in bowl 2 with an electric beater or stand mixer for 1–2 minutes. Scrape around the sides to make sure all is incorporated.

Add the liquid ingredients and mix well until all the ingredients are incorporated – about 1–2 minutes. Add the pecans and stir in gently. Cover with plastic wrap and chill for at least 2 hours. Remove from fridge and leave at room temperature for 30 minutes. Roll into balls (using about 1 ½ tablespoons of batter).

Bake at 350°F for about 12–13 minutes. They may look uncooked and have a mound on top but remove from the oven and give the cookie sheet a couple of bangs. The mounds will drop and little cracks will appear in the cookie. Leave on the pan for about 5 minutes and then place on cookie rack to cool.

Maple Frosting

INGREDIENTS

2 tablespoons butter
⅓ cup maple syrup
1 ⅓ cups icing sugar

METHOD

Place butter and maple syrup in a saucepan.

Mix over medium heat until the butter is completely melted. Remove from heat and add icing sugar.

Work quickly with the frosting and place a dollop on the cookie or drizzle from a piping bag (or plastic sandwich bag with a small corner snipped off).

Featured Grandmother

Anna Ryan

"She has shared her passion and love of cooking and baking with all her family. She is so loved."

CLASSIC GINGER COOKIES

Anna Ryan's recipe

INGREDIENTS

¾ cup butter or margarine
1 cup white sugar (plus extra for rolling)
1 egg
½ cup molasses
2 ½ cups flour
1 ½ teaspoons baking soda
2 teaspoons cinnamon
2 teaspoons ginger
½ teaspoon cloves

METHOD

In a large bowl, cream together the butter and sugar until light and fluffy. Add the egg and mix well. Stir in the molasses until fully combined.

In a separate bowl, whisk together the flour, baking soda, cinnamon, ginger, and cloves. Gradually add the dry ingredients to the wet mixture, stirring until a soft dough forms. Shape the dough into a ball and place in a bowl and refrigerate overnight (at least).

Preheat oven to 350°F. Take small pieces of dough and roll into balls. Roll each ball lightly in white sugar, then place on parchment-lined baking sheet. Flatten each ball slightly with a fork.

Bake for 10-12 minutes, or until the edges are set and the cookies have a slight crackle on top. Let cool on the baking sheet for a few minutes before removing from the pan and placing on cooling rack.

In the heart of Mulgrave, Nova Scotia, Anna Ryan's kitchen is more than just a place to cook — it's the centre of a lifetime of love, laughter, and family. At nearly 95 years old, with not a single gray hair on her head (a remarkable family trait), she carries herself with the warmth and wisdom of a woman who has spent decades nurturing those around her.

Her kitchen, always welcoming, is anchored by a gleaming old stove that radiates comforting heat. With a warming oven on top and a rocking chair nestled beside it, it's the perfect spot to gather, reflect, and enjoy the simple pleasures of home.

As a mother of 12 children, and grandmother of 30 and great-grandmother of 32, Anna's legacy is as rich and full as the loaves of bread she has lovingly baked over the years. Her kitchen has witnessed it all — joyful celebrations, quiet moments of reflection, shared meals, and the laughter of generations learning to cook at her side. She has passed down her love of baking and cooking to her family, ensuring that her traditions will live on through their hands and hearts.

Whether kneading dough, offering words of wisdom, or simply making space for family to gather, Anna's presence makes her kitchen the warm, beating heart of her home.

Anna's advice to her grandchildren: *"Happiness is homemade."*

QUICK OAT COOKIES

My sister Bernice Smith openly admits to not enjoying baking, but anything she bakes is always delicious. It took some nudging, but she came through with this recipe, and it has no egg in it. Easy and delicious.

INGREDIENTS

⅓ cup shortening
½ cup butter
1 cup brown sugar
1 teaspoon vanilla
1 teaspoon baking soda dissolved in 4 tablespoons hot water
1 ½ cups all-purpose flour
1 teaspoon salt
½ teaspoon nutmeg
2 cups rolled oats (quick oats)

METHOD

Mix the shortening, butter, sugar, and vanilla until creamed. Add the flour, salt, and nutmeg and mix well. Add the oats until blended. Form into balls and press down with a fork. Bake at 400°F for 8-10 minutes, or until nicely browned.

Featured Grandmother

Anna Isabel Connolly

"She whizzes around the kitchen, as she has always done, and makes sure we are all well fed."

GRANMOM'S CABIN COOKIES

Anna Isabel Connolly's recipe

INGREDIENTS

4 cups flour
1 teaspoon baking soda
1 teaspoon salt
¾ teaspoon ground cloves
1 cup melted shortening
1 cup sugar
1 cup molasses
2 eggs, beaten

METHOD

Place flour, baking soda, salt and cloves in a large bowl. In a separate bowl, melt shortening and then add sugar, molasses and eggs, and mix well. Add to the dry ingredients. If too sticky, add a little more flour. Roll into balls. Press with a fork. Bake for 10 minutes in 375°F oven.

Makes 4 dozen. Can press thinner for crisper cookie.

From the moment I walked into the facility where Anna Isabel Connolly now lives, it was clear she was no ordinary resident. Dressed in her Sunday best, radiating warmth and charm, she welcomed me with a conversation so full of life that I nearly forgot she wasn't in her own kitchen. Though her knees may no longer cooperate, her spirit is as strong as ever. Her granddaughter's heartfelt nomination tells the story of a woman whose love, generosity, and home-cooked meals shaped an entire family—and even now, she remains the heart of it all.

Married to her beloved husband for 58 years until his passing in 2013, she raised 11 children, welcomed 36 grandchildren, and has an ever-growing number of great-grandchildren. Most of them still live within a few kilometres of each other, a testament to the closeness she nurtured.

Her grandchildren can often be found confiding in her and for sure, they get the best of advice and most often, come away with a good story and a few laughs. For decades, her home was the family's gathering place, where a steaming pot of beef and barley soup was always on the stove, accompanied by fresh bread, biscuits, and molasses cookies — every single day. Christmas dinners for 50-plus people were simply routine, and no one ever left her home without full bellies and warm wool mittens or stocking caps she had made herself.

Though she now lives in a nursing home, she doesn't rest — she looks after others, just as she always has. And when she visits home, she's right back in the kitchen, making sure her family is well-fed, proving that love, like a good pot of soup, only deepens with time.

Anna's advice to her grandchildren: *"Remember – kindness will take you further than anything else in life."*

SPICY OATMEAL RAISIN COOKIES

An old-fashioned cookie – if you like raisins and cinnamon, this is for you!

INGREDIENTS

1 cup butter or margarine
1 cup brown sugar
½ cup white sugar
2 eggs
1 teaspoon vanilla
1 ½ cups flour
1 teaspoon baking soda
1 teaspoon cinnamon
½ teaspoon cloves
½ teaspoon salt
3 cups rolled oats
1 cup raisins

METHOD

Mix ingredients in the order given. Drop a small scoop or tablespoon onto a parchment-lined cookie sheet. Bake at 350°F for 10 minutes, or until brown around the edges.

Featured Grandmother

Sharon Tayes

"She loves to bake cookies for me – my favourite are the ones with jam in the middle. I just love her!"

Sharon's advice to her grandchildren: *"Live, Laugh, and Love."*

The warm, comforting scent of cinnamon greeted me even before Sharon Tayes opened the door to her beautifully adorned home in Saint John, New Brunswick. Though every room was inviting, the kitchen was the loveliest place to be — where tea was poured, stories were shared, and family gathered. Her daughter, Amanda, and grandson, Wyatt, who proudly nominated her, joined us for the visit. On the counter sat a spread of soft molasses cookies, each with a perfect dimple of jam in the centre — her husband's absolute favourite.

Sharon believes that a home should reflect the way you live, and when she dreams up an improvement, her husband, with his talent for design and carpentry, brings it to life. But no matter how beautiful the home, it's her warmth and kindness that make it truly special. She works by day at a daycare, ensuring children feel just as nurtured as her own grandchildren (Wyatt, Kyron, and Madelyn), who are always treated to home-cooked meals and fresh-baked treats.

When winter's chill sets in, Sharon loves escaping to places where the sun is hot and the scenery breathtaking, but no matter where she travels, home is where her heart truly shines. Whether she's baking, caring for her beloved pets — two beautiful dogs and two cats — or simply making those around her feel cherished, Sharon embodies kindness and grace. Beautiful inside and out, she fills her home with love, laughter, and the irresistible scent of something wonderful baking in the oven.

MOLASSES JAM GEMS

Sharon Tayes' recipe

INGREDIENTS

1 cup molasses
½ cup white sugar
½ cup shortening
1 egg
2 cups flour
½ teaspoon salt
1 teaspoon ginger
1 teaspoon cloves
1 teaspoon cinnamon
⅓ cup milk
2 teaspoons vinegar
2 teaspoons baking soda

METHOD

Mix wet ingredients well.

Mix the dry ingredients and add to the molasses mixture.

In a small bowl, mix the remaining ingredients and add to the rest of the batter. Form into a ball. Roll out to about ¼ inch thickness and cut with a 3-inch cookie cutter.

These cookies can be baked just like this or make a thumbprint in the centre and add your favourite jam.

Bake at 350°F for 10-15 minutes.

Featured Grandmother

Carole's advice to her grandchildren: *"Always leave a place better than you found it – whether it's a kitchen, a heart, or the world."*

Carole Regan

A hostess with grace and polish in a life that placed her in the public eye for many years. This delightful grandmother deserves to be in the limelight once again, but this time as a treasured mother and grandmother.

CAROLE'S BUTTERSCOTCH OATMEAL BARS

Carole Regan's recipe

INGREDIENTS

1 cup butter (softened but without melting)
1 teaspoon vanilla
1 ¼ cups brown sugar
4 ¼ cups rolled oats
Chopped pecans, almond slices (optional)

METHOD

Combine the butter and stir in the brown sugar and vanilla and cream well. Add the oats and mix well until it all comes together. Press into a 9x13-inch pan (lined with parchment paper). Bake at 325°F for 30 minutes. Cut while warm. Delicious.

Carole Regan is the kind of grandmother everyone wishes they had — warm, welcoming, and effortlessly elegant. The wife of former Nova Scotia Premier Gerald Regan, Carole is a mother of six children and a proud grandmother to 13.

Renowned for her gracious hosting, she has a special gift for making guests feel at home and, more impressively, for creating a feast on a moment's notice. When I arrived at her beautiful home, she met me at the door with a smile, and we spent time reminiscing about days gone by. It was a gathering filled with laughter, stories, and music.

My children, Brennan and Kelly, along with Brennan's daughter, Anna, who perform together as the band Kinna — meaning "family"—joined us and sang a few songs, making the visit even more special. Carole's daughter Nancy Regan, a dear friend of mine, is an accomplished author and television personality, and the entire Regan family shares a legacy of talent and warmth.

Now enjoying retirement, Carole continues to embrace life with joy, surrounded by the love of her family. She generously shared a recipe that has stood the test of time —her famous butterscotch oat bars. Outrageously simple yet irresistibly delicious, they have long been a favourite in her household, delighting generations. Carole's life is a testament to the beauty of family, friendship, and the magic that happens when love and good food come together.

OMG – COOKIE BUTTER COOKIES

A recipe from my friend, Debbie MacDonald

INGREDIENTS

½ cup butter (room temperature)
½ cup cookie butter spread, plus extra cookie butter for the cookie tops
⅔ cup light brown sugar, packed
1 large egg (room temperature)
1 teaspoon vanilla
1 ½ cups plus 1 tablespoon all-purpose flour
½ teaspoon salt
½ teaspoon baking soda
(Pecans or walnuts optional)

METHOD

Preheat oven to 350°F.

Mix the butter, cookie butter, and brown sugar until fluffy. Stir in the egg and vanilla. Mix in the flour, salt, and baking soda. Scoop the dough with a large cookie/ice cream scoop onto a parchment-lined cookie sheet – spacing them 3 inches apart. Add 1 teaspoon of cookie butter on top of each dough ball. Bake for 12 minutes or until the edges are golden and the melted cookie butter is crackled. Let cool completely on a wire rack and then enjoy.

Makes 1 dozen cookies. I'd double it if I were you!!

Featured Grandmother

Maureen Sutherland

"Nan takes us on non-stop adventures."

PEGGY'S COCONUT SQUARES

Maureen Sutherland's recipe

INGREDIENTS

Base:
¾ cup butter
½ cup brown sugar
1 ½ cups flour
1 egg yolk

Top:
2 eggs (whipped)
1 cup brown sugar
½ teaspoon vanilla
½ teaspoon almond extract
2 ½ tablespoons flour
¼ teaspoon salt
½ teaspoon baking powder
1 cup coconut
½ cup chopped cherries

Icing:
2 ½ cups icing sugar
½ cup soft butter
¼ teaspoon salt
½-¾ teaspoon each of vanilla and almond extract
1 ¾ tablespoons milk

Blend well with electric beater and spread over squares. Enjoy.

METHOD

Blend base ingredients well and press into a 9x9-inch pan. Bake at 350°F for 20 minutes.

Combine top ingredients and beat well with electric beater and then slowly add the dry ingredients.

Spread over base and bake at 350°F for 20–25 minutes until set. Cool and ice with butter icing.

Walking into Maureen Sutherland's home in Howie Centre, Nova Scotia, felt like stepping into the heart of a celebration. Greeted by her at the door, I was introduced to her husband, a couple of her lovely grandchildren, and a whole bunch of her spirited sisters. I immediately thought, *This is the place to be when there's a party!*

Laughter filled the air, and the dining room table was a feast for the eyes — set with elegant dinnerware, fine bone china cups and saucers, and an irresistible spread of homemade treats. It was the kind of gathering that made you want to pull up a chair and stay awhile.

Maureen is a grandmother who refuses to sit still. With her five grandchildren in tow, she explores every beach imaginable, introducing them to the breathtaking beauty of the ocean. She takes them around the Cabot Trail, on hikes, berry-picking adventures, and even camping trips. Her love for nature is something she shares with passion, ensuring they experience all the wonders Cape Breton has to offer.

But beyond the adventures, Maureen's heart is in her kitchen. Along with her sisters, she treasures the recipes passed down through generations, each one a link to their family's history. The recipe she shares in this book is particularly special — it comes from a beloved family friend who has passed, Peggy, a testament to the traditions that bind them all together.

Vibrant, generous, and full of life, Maureen makes every person who steps into her home feel like part of the family.

Maureen's advice to her grandchildren: *"Practice having an attitude of gratitude."*

SHORTBREAD TREATS

I made these on Tunes and Wooden Spoons (Facebook *livestream) with guest Tyler White. This recipe is my go-to if I take squares anywhere.*

INGREDIENTS

1 cup butter (softened)
1 cup brown sugar
1 egg yolk
1 teaspoon vanilla
2 cups flour
1 teaspoon salt
6 Aero bars
Chopped pecans
1 Skor bar (chopped finely)

METHOD

Mix butter and brown sugar, add the egg yolk and vanilla and mix well. Add flour and salt and use your hands to combine into a doughy ball. Drop by chunks into a parchment-lined 9x13 pan and bake at 350°F for 25 minutes only.

Remove from oven and immediately place 6 chocolate bars on top of the hot base. Allow the chocolate to naturally melt (for about 5 minutes) and then spread. Sprinkle with chopped pecans and chopped Skor bar bits.

Let cool until the chocolate sets and cut into squares. This may take a couple of hours for the chocolate to set. Near the end of this time, I usually place them in the fridge for about 30 minutes in order to allow the chocolate to properly set. Remove from the pan by sliding a knife along the edges or lifting them out if you've used parchment paper. Slices perfectly into bar-style squares. Keeps nicely in the fridge and also freezes well. I like them better if left on the counter until they reach room temperature so that the base softens a bit.

Featured Grandmother

Rita's advice to her grandchildren: "Faire le bien contre le mal. (Do good against evil.)"

Rita Benoit

"Through her cooking, she has embedded our culture in us and fostered a deep love of food. She is not just a cook; she is a beloved matriarch, a community cornerstone, and a keeper of our family traditions."

RITA'S BEST BROWNIES

Rita Benoit's recipe

INGREDIENTS

½ cup plus 2 tablespoons margarine
1 cup granulated sugar
1 teaspoon vanilla
5 tablespoons cocoa
2 eggs
½ cup all-purpose flour

Frosting:
5 tablespoons soft butter
5 tablespoons cocoa
1 ½ cups icing sugar
1 teaspoon vanilla
2 tablespoons milk

METHOD

Combine first four ingredients. Add the eggs and mix well. Add flour and mix until blended. Pour into an 8-inch square pan and bake at 325°F for 30 minutes. Let cool.

Mix all frosting ingredients together until you meet the desired consistency. Spread on cooled brownies and sprinkle with chopped walnuts. So delicious.

Spending time with Rita Benoit in her Pomquet, Nova Scotia, home was an experience I won't soon forget — mostly because my cheeks were sore from laughing so much! A true comedian, Rita's quick wit and infectious humour filled the room, making it clear that joy is just as much a part of her home as the incredible food she prepares. A proud Acadian grandmother, she has spent her life nurturing her family, not just with love, but with the warmth of home-cooked meals and cherished traditions.

Rita is the youngest of 14 children, raised by a hardworking mother who instilled in her the values of resilience and dedication. These qualities have shaped her life, making her the heart and soul of both her family and her community. A lifelong member of the Pomquet Ladies Club and a dedicated contributor to the Pomquet Development Société, Rita's culinary talents have fed generations — her famous meat pies and fricot with dumplings are legendary.

Her love of baking is equally renowned. Rita's brownies are so beloved they've been known to fetch high prices at auctions, and her holiday tradition of preparing up to 15 platters of homemade treats is a testament to her generosity. Until recently, she made over 100 meat pies each Christmas, ensuring her family was well-fed in the most delicious way possible.

More than just a cook, Rita is a matriarch, a keeper of Acadian traditions, and, without a doubt, the glue that holds her family together.

CRUNCHY LEMON SQUARES

I LOVE these squares. A definite keeper!

INGREDIENTS

1 cup rolled oats
1 cup flour
½ cup coconut
½ cup walnuts
½ cup packed brown sugar
1 teaspoon baking powder
½ cup melted butter or margarine
1 can Eagle Brand condensed milk
½ cup lemon juice

METHOD

Combine the rolled oats, flour, coconut, nuts, sugar, baking powder, and butter. Mix well until crumbly. Pat ½ mixture in a 9x9-inch pan. Set the rest aside. Mix the sweet milk and lemon juice and pour over mixture in pan and cover with the remaining mixture. Pat lightly. Bake at 350°F for 25 minutes, or until lightly browned.

MILLIONAIRE SHORTBREAD SQUARES

I make these ALL the time – absolutely the best.

INGREDIENTS

Base:
¾ cup butter (room temperature)
¾ cup brown sugar
1 egg yolk
½ teaspoon salt
1 teaspoon vanilla
2 cups flour

Caramel Layer:
½ cup butter (room temperature makes it faster)
1 cup light brown sugar
½ teaspoon salt
¼ cup corn syrup (light or dark)
1 can sweetened condensed milk
1 teaspoon vanilla

METHOD

You will need a 9x9-inch square pan – prepared with parchment paper that is cut to size and with an overhang which will be used to "lift" your finished squares out for cutting.

With an electric beater, cream the butter and then add the sugar. Beat. Add the egg yolk, salt, and vanilla, and beat until combined. Add only 1 cup of the flour and beat. Add the second cup and mix on slow until just combined. Place into your prepared pan and press down until smooth.

Bake at 350°F for about 22 minutes until just brown along the edges.

Put the caramel layer ingredients (EXCEPT THE VANILLA) into a saucepan over medium heat and use a whisk. It's best to have a thermometer that must reach a temperature of 225°F. Once the temperature is reached, you will then add the vanilla.

When the base comes out of the oven, it's okay to pour the caramel right over it and spread it out evenly. Place in the refrigerator for 10 minutes.

Chocolate Ganache

INGREDIENTS

⅓ cup whipping cream
1 ½ cups semi-sweet chocolate chips

METHOD

You have a few options here on how to prepare the ganache. Place in a bowl and place over the top of a pot with very hot water and let the chocolate melt; OR melt in the microwave using half-power and in 30-second bursts (stirring after each 30 seconds); OR scald the whipping cream, pour over the chocolate chips and let it sit for a minute – and then stir.

Pour over the caramel layer and spread out. Refrigerate until chocolate is set. Don't try to cut them while the chocolate is "almost" set – wait until the chocolate is hard. This may take a couple of hours. "Lift" the squares out of the pan using the "handles" of parchment paper. Slice with a good sharp, large knife. Best kept in a plastic container in the fridge. (They also freeze well.) Enjoy!

Featured Grandfather

Jim Evans

"Geegaw feeds his grandchildren with his yummy baked goods and takes pride in regularly surprising friends, family, and service providers with his famous treats."

FUDGE SQUARES

Jim Evans' recipe

INGREDIENTS

½ cup butter (or margarine)
1 cup brown sugar
1 egg
A dash of salt
1 cup flour
1 teaspoon baking powder

Frosting:
1 cup brown sugar
¼ cup milk
4 tablespoons soft butter
1 cup icing sugar
1 teaspoon vanilla

METHOD

Combine and spread in a 9x9-inch pan. Bake for 20 minutes at 350°F.

Combine frosting ingredients in a saucepan and bring to a boil and continue to boil for 2 minutes.

Remove from the stove and add icing sugar and vanilla

Beat well with an electric beater. Pour over the base.

After 20 minutes, cut into squares with a knife dipped in hot water. Absolutely delicious.

When I decided to include two grandfathers in this book, my first choice was easy — the grandpa who asked, "What about grandpas?"

But my second choice came to me just as quickly: Jim Evans. A longtime supporter of *Tunes and Wooden Spoons* since its very beginning in 2020, Jim has not only been a loyal follower but also one of the most fun and enthusiastic. I'll never forget the Halloween when he posted a photo of himself dressed up as me — wig, red lipstick, *Tunes and Wooden Spoons* apron, and all! How could I not pick Jim?

But beyond his sense of humour, Jim is a man who truly embodies the spirit of generosity. He is a passionate cook and baker, always showing his love through food. When he attends a gathering, he doesn't just bring one dish — he brings dozens, making sure everyone is well-fed and appreciated. Whether it's to celebrate others or to say thank you, Jim's food is always made with care and kindness.

A devoted husband, father, and grandfather — affectionately known as "Geegaw" — Jim's heart is as big as his batches of baked goods. Now, finally retired after many years of hard work, he and his wife Patsy are looking forward to travelling and celebrating this next chapter of life. If there's one thing I know for sure, wherever they go, Jim will find a way to spread joy — most likely with a plate of homemade treats in hand.

Jim's advice to his grandchildren: *"My mom's baking has always inspired me to bake. I hope my baking inspires my children and grandchildren to continue the tradition. Baking with them is a second chance to do it all over again. Their smiles say it all."*

GERRY'S FUDGE

Gerry Giroux Jr. visited my home with his parents, Gerry Sr. and wife Wilma. They live in Ontario and were visiting Cape Breton to go to a wedding for a relative in Glace Bay. They had my cookbooks and wanted them signed. Gerry Jr. spoke of how he makes a simple fudge for his children's teams on a regular basis, and he shared this simple recipe for the most delicious fudge I've ever tasted.

INGREDIENTS

1 cup butter (cubed) or margarine
2 cups brown sugar
1 can sweetened condensed milk (300 ml)
1 cup white chocolate chips
1 teaspoon vanilla

METHOD

Place the butter, sugar, and milk in a microwaveable bowl and microwave for 11 minutes (stirring at 2-minute intervals).

Remove from microwave and with an electric beater, beat in white chocolate chips and vanilla until combined (about 1 minute).

Pour into a buttered 9-inch square pan (metal, glass, or Pyrex), OR, pour into an un-buttered silicone 9-inch square pan. Refrigerate for a couple of hours and cut into squares.

Chocolate Fudge – instead of white chocolate chips, use chocolate chips, along with chopped walnuts or pecans.

Featured Grandmother

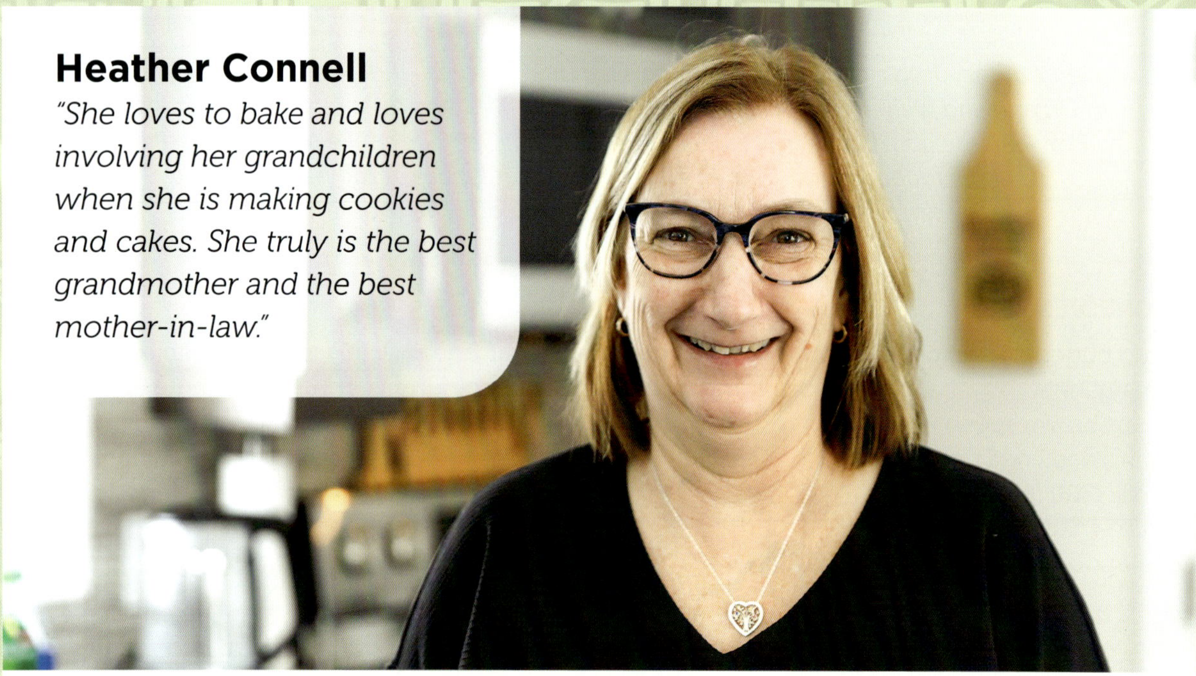

Heather Connell

"She loves to bake and loves involving her grandchildren when she is making cookies and cakes. She truly is the best grandmother and the best mother-in-law."

Heather Connell welcomed us into her Miramichi, New Brunswick, home with open arms, and from the moment we arrived, we knew we were in for a wonderful visit. Her dear mother, well into her nineties, joined us, and she was an absolute delight. Surrounded by family, with her grandchildren adding an extra dose of joy, it was clear that Heather's home is one filled with love and laughter.

I had often noticed Heather's name in the comments on my *Facebook* page, so when her daughter-in-law nominated her, I knew she had to be part of this book — her enthusiasm and support had already made her feel like a friend.

True to Maritime hospitality, Heather had her table filled with treats for everyone to enjoy, and of course, a good, hot cup of tea. But the highlight? Her caramel fudge. Before I even realized what I was doing, I had polished off three pieces — it was just that good!

Her daughter-in-law's nomination spoke volumes about the kind of grandmother and mother-in-law she is, carrying on the cherished tradition of weekly Sunday family dinners, now with her own grandchildren, ensuring there are always plenty of leftovers and sweet treats to go around.

Heather had even shared her cinnamon bread recipe in my last cookbook! A gracious host, full of energy, and with a home impeccably kept (though she's far too busy for pictures!), she was a joy to visit. Heather, next time, come to Cape Breton — I'll make YOU sit down for a change!

CREAMY CARAMEL FUDGE

Heather Connell's recipe

INGREDIENTS

⅔ cup evaporated milk
3 cups white sugar
¾ cup butter
2 cups miniature marshmallows
4 ½ milk chocolate caramel bars
½ teaspoon vanilla

METHOD

Put the sugar, milk, and butter in saucepan and bring to a boil, stirring constantly. Continue to boil for 5 minutes, stirring constantly. Remove from heat and add marshmallows and vanilla until the marshmallows have melted. Add the chocolate bars and beat until smooth with electric beater.

Line a 10x13-inch pan with parchment paper or foil and pour in the fudge batter. Let cool before cutting. So delicious.

Heather's advice to her grandchildren: *"Always stay humble and kind while reaching for your goals".*

CARAMEL CONES

Tasted this delicious treat at my friend Sheila Johnston's in New Waterford. It is so hard to have just one! She loves to keep them in her freezer and serve them to the neighbourhood children.

INGREDIENTS

1 can sweetened condensed milk
1 cup butter
2 cups brown sugar
1 250-gram bag mini marshmallows
1 box of 42 mini ice-cream cones

METHOD

Put the first four ingredients in a microwavable bowl and stir. Microwave for 8 minutes, stopping to stir every 2 minutes. Pour into cones immediately. Keep at room temperature until set and then refrigerate or freeze.

CARAMEL TURTLE BROWNIE SQUARES

This recipe is from Christina MacDonell, in memory of her grandmother Cassie MacDonell who entertained visitors by the hundreds when they came to visit her husband, affectionately known as "Little Collie." Collie welcomed those who were searching for their family tree information, and he loved to tell stories. Cassie was always a gracious host and I've had a few good cups of tea with her over the years. Hers was a welcoming kitchen with the smells of goodies baking and a big pot of tea on the stove. This particular recipe was a favourite of her grandchildren.

INGREDIENTS

¼ cup butter
2 eggs
2 ounces semi-sweet chocolate
1 cup sugar
½ teaspoon vanilla
¼ teaspoon salt
½ cup flour
½ cup pecan halves
¾ cup semi-sweet chocolate chips

METHOD

Butter an 8-inch square pan. In small saucepan, melt butter and chocolate together then set aside. In a medium bowl, beat eggs, sugar, salt, and vanilla. Stir in the melted chocolate mixture, then the flour. Pour into pan and bake at 350°F for 15 minutes.

Remove pan from oven and top with pecan halves and caramel syrup (recipe below). Bake for another 15 minutes. Remove from oven and immediately sprinkle with the chocolate chips. Gently swirl the surface with a knife.

Caramel Syrup

½ cup butter
⅓ cup brown sugar

Bring butter and sugar to a boil in a small saucepan, stirring constantly for 1 minute.

HOODIE'S TURTLE CHOCOLATES

In memory of a leatherback turtle I found on the beach in Port Hood in 2024. The Canadian Sea Turtle Network had it picked up and sent to a lab, but after a couple of days, it was determined that it had passed away. It was a beautiful creature, and the network named him "Hoodie" after the place he was found. These little gems are named in Hoodie's honour.

INGREDIENTS

- 6 tablespoon butter
- ½ cup brown sugar
- ½ cup white sugar
- ½ cup sweetened condensed milk
- ½ cup light corn syrup
- ½ teaspoon vanilla
- 2 cups unsalted peanuts (or pecan halves) chopped
- 1 package semi-sweet chocolate chips
- 1 package butterscotch chips

METHOD

In a microwavable bowl, melt the butter for about 30-40 seconds. Stir in both sugars, sweetened condensed milk, and corn syrup, then return the bowl to the microwave for 6-8 minutes, or until the mixture reaches 235°F on an instant-read thermometer. Once ready, stir in the vanilla and chopped nuts. Drop large spoons of the caramel mixture onto a parchment-lined baking sheet and refrigerate for 20 minutes.

Meanwhile, melt the chocolate and butterscotch chips in the microwave on half-power, stirring every couple of minutes until smooth (about 4-5 minutes). Stir well to combine. Using a fork, dip each caramel cluster into the melted chocolate mixture, then place them back on the parchment paper. Return to the refrigerator to set, then store in an airtight container.

This recipe makes about 20 turtles. For a fun touch, I added extra peanuts after dipping to create little heads and feet for the turtles.

DESSERTS AND CAKES

RUSTIC APPLE GALETTE

Chef Sharon MacEachern from Judique made this on Tunes and Wooden Spoons.

INGREDIENTS

Pie Crust:
1 ½ cups flour
½ teaspoon salt
3 tablespoons sugar
¾ cup cold butter
¼ cup coldest water

Filling:
4–5 apples (Granny Smith, Gala, or Honey Crisp)
⅓ cup brown sugar
1 teaspoon vanilla
2 teaspoons cinnamon
2 tablespoons melted butter
Dash of salt

METHOD

Line a baking sheet with parchment paper. Combine the flour, salt, and sugar and add the cold butter and mix with your hands (or a pastry blender or food processor) until the butter is the size of peas. Sprinkle the cold water over the mixture until it is crumbly and the dough forms.

Transfer the dough to a lightly floured work surface and bring it together into a cohesive ball. Pat the dough into a disk. Flour your work surface and dust the dough with flour and using a rolling pin, roll into a circle about 8 to 10 inches in diameter, turning and adding more flour as necessary so the dough doesn't stick. Refrigerate while you prepare the filling.

Peel, core, and cut apples into 1/8-inch slices (you should have about 4 cups apples) and place in a large bowl.

Add remaining ingredients and toss all to combine. Set aside.

Take the dough from the fridge and slide the parchment paper onto the countertop. Roll the dough directly onto the parchment paper into a 14-inch circle about 1/8 inch thick. It's fine if the edges are a little ragged. Place the parchment and dough back on the baking sheet – the pastry should curve up the lip of the pan.

Assemble the Tart:

Sprinkle 1 tablespoon flour evenly over the pastry. Arrange the apple slices on top in overlapping concentric circles to within 3 inches of the edge. Don't worry about making it look perfect! It doesn't make much difference in the end, and you don't want the dough to get too warm. Fold the edges of the dough over the apples in a free-form fashion, working your way around and creating pleats as you go. Patch up any tears by pinching a bit of dough from the edge.

Brush the edges with egg wash (1 egg and a tablespoon of cold water, beaten with a fork) and apply with a pastry brush. Sprinkle with sugar.

Bake at 350°F for 30-40 minutes or until apples are tender. Serve with caramel sauce and ice cream.

Featured Grandmother

Elizabeth Beaton

"Known as the Pie Lady to many, Elizabeth (Nana) has been a staple of the Mabou Farmers Market since its inception. She always brings pies for any occasion and often drops off one or two to us every time she visits!"

ELIZABETH'S APPLE PIE

Elizabeth Beaton's recipe

INGREDIENTS

Pastry:
2 cups flour
2/3 cup shortening
1 teaspoon salt
3 tablespoons ice water

Filling:
5 cups sliced apples
2/3 cup sugar
2 tablespoons cornstarch
3/4 teaspoon cinnamon

METHOD

Prepare the filling by mixing the flour, cornstarch, and cinnamon and then toss with the apples. Set aside.

In a mixing bowl, combine the flour and salt for the pastry. Work the shortening into the flour until the mixture has pea-sized clumps. Sprinkle the ice water over the flour mixture and gently work with a fork and/or hands until the dough forms into a ball. Do not overwork. Divide the dough in two, with one part being slightly larger than the other for the bottom crust. Roll out the bottom crust and gently place in a 10-inch pie plate. Spread the filling over the bottom crust. Roll out the top crust and place over the apples. There should be a small amount of pastry overhang around the edge of the pie. Fold it under and flute (or press with fork tines). Slit the crust to allow steam to escape. For a golden crust, brush lightly with milk.

Bake at 400°F for 30 minutes and then reduce the heat to 350°F for another 20 to 25 minutes or until the apples are soft when pierced with a fork and the crust is golden.

Elizabeth Beaton's life has been one of dedication — to her students, to her family, to her community, and now, to the art of baking the perfect pie. Living most of her married life in Glencoe, Cape Breton, she spent her career shaping young minds as an elementary school teacher, guiding each student with a heart full of gold and a hand full of love. Now retired, she hasn't strayed far from home, settling just down the road in picturesque Southwest Mabou, where she continues to share her gifts with those around her.

A passionate supporter of Cape Breton's musical traditions, Elizabeth has been instrumental in keeping the legendary square dances of Glencoe alive. On any given Thursday night throughout the summer, she can be found at the old schoolhouse, either behind the counter serving tea or goodies, or seated among friends, soaking in the joyous energy of fiddles and footwork that make the floor come alive.

While her family has long known her as a gifted cook, the rest of the community has come to know her as "The Pie Lady" of the Mabou Farmers' Market. For the past seventeen years, eager customers have lined up before she even arrives, hoping to take home one of her delicious homemade pies — some adorned with a signature happy face in the crust, a touch of warmth that makes them all the more special. At 90 years young, Elizabeth embraces a life of calm, family joy, and deep community connection, with her beloved children, grandsons, and great-grandchildren never far from her heart.

Elizabeth's advice to her grandchildren: *"To my grandsons – My one regret is that I never taught you how to iron a shirt, but it's not too late! You can still sign up!"*

LEMON BLUEBERRY CUSTARD PIE

A lemony custard – light and fluffy

INGREDIENTS

1 tablespoon butter
⅔ cup white sugar
3 tablespoons lemon juice
2 tablespoons flour
1 tablespoon lemon zest
2 egg yolks
1 cup milk
2 egg whites
9-inch unbaked pie crust
1 ¾ cups fresh blueberries

METHOD

Preheat oven to 350°F. Cream the butter and add the sugar, flour, juice, lemon zest and mix well. Add the yolks and the milk and whisk.

Beat the egg whites until soft peaks form and then fold into the lemon mixture.

Pour the filling into the pie crust and then scatter the blueberries over the top.

Bake for 30 minutes at 350 and then cover loosely with foil and continue baking for an additional 25 minutes. The pie should jiggle a little when removing from oven. Set on cooling rack for at least 30 minutes before serving so that the custard will set.

Featured Grandmother

Lois MacIsaac

"Grandma Lois is a class act – you can see and taste the love she puts into anything she makes."

BUTTERSCOTCH PIE

Lois MacIsaac's recipe

INGREDIENTS

Filling:

2 rounded tablespoons butter
2 rounded tablespoons flour
1 cup brown sugar
Pinch of salt
3 beaten egg yolks
2 ½ cups milk
1 teaspoon vanilla

Meringue:

4 large egg whites (room temperature)
¼ teaspoon cream of tartar
⅓ cup white sugar

METHOD

Place brown sugar and butter in a large, heavy-bottomed saucepan and set heat to medium-low. In a small bowl, mix eggs yolks and milk together. Add the flour and mix well. Add to the saucepan with the sugar and butter and whisk until no lumps of flour or sugar remain. Turn heat to medium and cook, stirring frequently, until mixture is thick, like pudding. Remove from heat and add vanilla. Pour filling into blind-baked (pre-baked) deep dish pie 8–9-inch pie shell.

Beat egg whites and cream of tartar until soft peaks form. Slowly beat in the sugar until stiff peaks form. Spoon onto the pie. Bake in a 400°F oven for 5-6 minutes until the meringue is toasty brown.

Stepping through the door of Lois MacIsaac's century-old home in Dunvegan, Nova Scotia, felt like stepping into a warm embrace. The house, once belonging to her parents-in-law, has been lovingly cared for — preserving its history while reflecting Lois' own elegant touch. A self-described former city girl, she has fully embraced country life, creating a space that radiates both charm and calm.

From the well-tended flower gardens she adores to the cozy kitchen where we shared a slice of her exquisite butterscotch pie, everything about Lois speaks to beauty, tradition, and grace.

A "classy lady" in every sense—her style extends beyond fashion into the finesse with which she cooks, entertains, and tells stories. The small wood-burning stove in her kitchen, nestled between two windows and paired with a welcoming rocking chair, is the perfect backdrop for both conversation and quiet moments of reflection. There is a serenity about Lois, a peacefulness that comes from someone who has truly found home.

Beyond her kitchen and garden, Lois is deeply committed to her community. Her tireless work with the hospital's ladies' auxiliary is just one example of her generosity, and her dedication to the annual Broadcove Scottish Concert helps preserve and celebrate the rich Gaelic traditions of Cape Breton.

A devoted grandmother, an exceptional cook, and a treasured friend to many, Lois MacIsaac embodies warmth, kindness, and quiet strength. Anyone lucky enough to know her knows just how special she truly is.

Lois' advice to her grandchildren: *"Take time to enjoy life, especially your children – it all goes by so quickly. Enjoy it all."*

RHUBARB PIE WITH CRUMB TOPPING

This recipe is in memory of the late Gertrude Ada Ferguson from Prince Edward Island, a beloved lady who passed away before I was slated to visit with her in March. Gertrude lived her entire life in the Crapaud, Hampton area of Prince Edward Island where she raised four children. She was the first licensed female Emergency Medical Technician in PEI, then worked for Canada Post, all while raising her family and running a small hobby farm. On January 10, 2025, at the age of 91, Gertrude passed away. We trust she is now with the love of her life, her late husband, Sheldon Ferguson.

INGREDIENTS

Pie Filling:

1 ½ cups brown sugar
2 eggs
2 tablespoons water or milk
3 tablespoons flour
¼ teaspoon Salt
Dash of nutmeg
3 cups cut-up rhubarb (use the pink parts for a sweeter pie)

Crumb Top:

1 cup flour
½ cup brown sugar
½ cup butter

Gertrude's Rhubarb Sauce

½ cup white sugar
1 cup rhubarb
1 cup water
1 small packet gelatin

Place the sugar, rhubarb, and water in a saucepan and bring to a boil and then simmer for 15 minutes. Add the packet of gelatin and stir well and remove from heat. Let cool to room temperature.

METHOD

Combine pie ingredients in a large bowl and mix. Once combined, put it into a prepared single unbaked pie crust. Mix the crumb topping and put over the pie filling.

Preheat oven to 375°F. Place pie on a baking sheet and bake for 60 minutes. If the crust browns too early, cover it loosely with foil.

Cool before serving and serve with a dollop of whipped cream or vanilla ice cream or prepare some of Gertrude's rhubarb sauce to drizzle over top.

Featured Grandmother

Muriel Daley

"She is an amazing soul, caring, kind, and loving. She loves to spend time cooking for her children and making her grandchildren's favourite goodies."

NANA'S COCONUT CREAM PIE (WITH GF OPTION)

Muriel Daley's recipe

INGREDIENTS

2 cups all-purpose flour (GF option: 2 cups GF flour mixed with 1 ⅓ teaspoon xanthan gum and 4 tablespoons rice flour)
4 tablespoons white sugar
1 cup cold butter (grated)
1 ½ cup chopped pecans

Filling:
3 ¾ tablespoons cornstarch
¾ teaspoon salt
2 ¾ cups white sugar
4 cups whole milk
6 large (or extra-large) egg yolks beaten (saving whites)
1 ½ tablespoons butter
1 ½ teaspoons vanilla
1 ¼ cups sweetened coconut flakes

Meringue:
6 egg whites
¾ cup white sugar

Muriel's advice to her grandchildren: *"Since kindness is free, my dears, sprinkle that stuff everywhere! – with love from Nana/Nandy xo"*

METHOD

Mix dry ingredients. Blend in grated butter with a pastry blender. Mix in the pecans. Press into an 11x14-inch pan. Bake at 350°F for 11 minutes. Alternatively, this will make three 9-inch pies or two 8x8-inch pans.

Whisk the cornstarch, salt, and sugar and put in a large saucepan with a heavy bottom with just 2 cups of cold milk and stir until smooth.

In a separate saucepan, warm the remaining 2 cups of milk. Gently whisk some of the warm milk into the beaten egg yolks and then add warm milk/egg mixture into the cornstarch/sugar/milk mixture in another saucepan. Cook over medium heat, whisking and watching until thickened. Add the butter, vanilla, and coconut while cooking a wee bit more. Set aside and prepare meringue.

Place on a cooling rack.

Beat egg whites in deep metal bowl well until they begin to appear somewhat dry and starting to take shape. Slowly add the sugar and continue to beat on high until all the sugar has been added. Meringue should be shiny with stiff peaks. Put the coconut filling onto the base and top with the meringue, making decorative peaks. Sprinkle with some coconut if desired.

Bake at 390°F for about 10–14 minutes until golden. Watch that the coconut doesn't burn on top. Remove from oven and place on cooling rack until it reaches room temperature before cutting. So delicious.

Muriel Daley, from the small and picturesque community of Janeville, New Brunswick, welcomed me with open arms, the kind of greeting that instantly makes one feel at home. She and her husband, Len, live with a breathtaking view of Bay Chaleur, and they make the most of every day, embracing the beauty around them and the people they love.

When I visited, their daughter Tammy — who lives just across the road — joined us for a wonderful meal prepared by Muriel, followed by her decadent coconut cream pie and a good cup of tea. To top it all off, Len quietly took the dishes away and cleaned up — now that's a good man!

Faithful to their church, devoted to their family, and always there for their neighbours, Muriel and Len are the heart of their community. Muriel cherishes sentimental treasures — special dishes passed down through family and friends, each with its own story, are lovingly displayed throughout her home. But even more treasured are the experiences she shares with her grandchildren — whether it's swimming in the bay, walking on the beach collecting driftwood and beach glass, or playing games together.

Her kitchen is a place of love, where she cooks up favourite meals whenever family visits, and where her famous "Berry Good Trifle" has become a beloved staple in both her home and her community.

With endless energy, a heart full of kindness, and a knack for storytelling, Muriel Daley is the kind of grandmother who makes the world a better place — one home-cooked meal, one shared memory, and one beautiful moment at a time.

PECAN PIE

Make your own favourite single pie crust and place in a 9-inch pie plate or tart pan (do not prick the bottom of the pie crust!!). My single pie crust recipe and special directions is on the following page.

INGREDIENTS

Filling:
4 tablespoons butter
1 cup dark corn syrup
⅓ cup packed brown sugar
¼ cup maple syrup
¾ teaspoon salt
2 teaspoons vanilla

3 eggs and 1 egg yolk
1 cup chopped pecans

METHOD

Place filling ingredients in a saucepan. Mix slightly, put on medium heat, and whisk until it starts to bubble and continue whisking for 3 minutes. Remove from heat and set aside for about 10 minutes. Add vanilla and whisk again to combine.

In a bowl, whisk eggs together. Slowly whisk them into the brown sugar mixture.

Add chopped pecans and gently mix.

Pour into cooled baked crust.

Place pecan halves around the edges of the pie (if desired). Place in a 350°F oven and bake for 40 minutes. After about 20 minutes of baking, place a piece of foil over the top (so pecans don't burn). Remove from oven and place on cooling rack. It may be a little jiggly in the centre but it will thicken as it cools.

Serve warm with a scoop of vanilla ice cream or a dollop of whipped cream.

PIE CRUST

INGREDIENTS

1 cup flour
½ teaspoon salt
⅓ cup shortening or butter
Mix until mealy and add
2½-3 tablespoons coldest water.

METHOD

Mix gently and roll out until about 12 inches in diameter and place in pie plate. Use a fork to press down the edges (or fold as you like). For this pie, do not prick the base of the pie crust with a fork because the filling is very, very liquidy and that will seep down through the holes and makes it very hard to extract a piece of pie when it's ready to be eaten. (Trust me – I did this, and it was messy!) It's best to place a piece of parchment over the pie crust and fill it with either purchased pie weights, OR use uncooked beans or chickpeas to weigh down. With the pie weights, it took about 25 minutes at 375°F to cook the pie crust.

If not using weights of any kind, bake at 375°F for about 19 minutes or until just lightly browned. (I prick the bottom with a fork when I'm making other cream pies – like lemon, coconut cream, banana cream, butterscotch, etc.) and bake the single crust at 375°F for about 17-19 minutes or until just lightly browned. Cool.

Featured Grandmother

Pauline Chisholm

"Our nanny could fill a cookbook with our favourite recipes."

Pauline's advice to her grandchildren:
"If I get an invite to go out somewhere, I'm not missing it – I'm going out! And you should remember to do the same!"

From the moment I stepped into Pauline Chisholm's home in Heatherton, Nova Scotia, I felt the warmth of both her hospitality and her kitchen. This gentle and welcoming woman had everything set up and ready to bake, her dining table adorned with beautiful dishes. She didn't just make her famous chocolate pudding brownie dessert for me that day — she also prepared her beloved Snow Pudding, a treat as delightful as she is.

Pauline, a devoted mother of eight, has always ensured her family was well-fed with home-cooked meals, often on a budget but never lacking in flavour or love. Her grandchildren have cherished growing up with the comforting aromas of her kitchen, where a hot meal or a delicious dessert was always waiting. Nothing beats Nanny Pauline's recipes, and she is now passing them down through the generations, ensuring her legacy of love through food lives on.

When Pauline isn't in the kitchen, she can be found at a local card game or dancing at a seniors' country dance. Her shortbread cookies are legendary, her dill pickles are a Christmas favourite, and her holiday gatherings once included rabbit pies and family debates over whose boiled dinner had just the right amount of salt. She never lets anyone leave hungry, and if you try, she'll make sure you reconsider with her signature humour. I know that for sure because it was hard to get out the door without sampling a few of her goodies – including those decadent shortbreads. I will be back for tea, Pauline!

CHOCOLATE PUDDING BROWNIE DESSERT

Pauline Chisholm's recipe

INGREDIENTS

Batter:
1 cup flour
½ cup white sugar
1 teaspoon baking powder
2 teaspoons softened butter
½ cup milk
2 tablespoons cocoa

Topping:
¾ cup white sugar
2 tablespoons cocoa
½ cup boiling water

METHOD

Preheat oven to 325°F. In a mixing bowl, combine flour, sugar, baking powder, butter, and cocoa. Add the milk and mix until a smooth batter forms. Pour the batter into a greased 8x8 baking dish, spreading it evenly but not too close to the edges. Prepare the topping by stirring together the sugar, cocoa, and hot water and gently pour the mixture over the batter. Do not mix. Bake for 25–30 minutes, or until the top is set and the pudding layer has formed beneath. Serve warm with ice cream or whipped frozen topping.

Featured Grandmother

Gloria Smith

"Gloria is an incredible woman and she is loved beyond measure."

BLUEBERRY CAKE WITH BUTTERSCOTCH SAUCE

Gloria Smith's recipe

INGREDIENTS

½ cup shortening
1 cup white sugar
2 eggs
1 teaspoon vanilla
2 cups flour
4 teaspoons baking powder
½ teaspoon salt
1 cup milk
1 cup fresh blueberries

Sauce:
1 cup brown sugar
3 cups hot water
Pinch of salt
1 tablespoon butter
1 teaspoon vanilla
Pinch of nutmeg (optional)
2 tablespoons cornstarch (in small amount of water)

METHOD

Mix the shortening, sugar, eggs, and vanilla until smooth. Mix the dry ingredients together and alternate mixing the dry ingredients and the milk until just combined. Pour into a greased 9x9 pan (or 9x11) pan. Bake at 350°F for about 35 minutes.

Bring the sugar, hot water, salt, butter, and vanilla to a boil. Remove from heat. Mix the cornstarch with enough cold water to make it liquid and stir into the hot mixture. Do not return to heat, just stir and it will thicken. Spread warm over a slice of cake when serving.

In the heart of Augustine Cove, Prince Edward Island, Gloria Smith has spent a lifetime nurturing, giving, and embodying the true meaning of family. From the moment I stepped into her warm and welcoming home, it felt like visiting a lifelong friend. There are no airs with Gloria — just kindness, authenticity, and a deep love for the people around her.

As the eldest of 10 siblings, Gloria learned early what it meant to work hard and care for others. She helped raise her younger brothers and sisters before raising her own family of four daughters. Her home has always been filled with love, laughter, and the comforting aromas of her home-cooked meals and baked goods. Her famous blueberry cake with sauce is a cherished staple at family gatherings, where her children and grandchildren ensure that every celebration is special.

Life has thrown many challenges Gloria's way. In recent months, she stood by her husband of over 50 years as he faced a life-altering amputation. And now, she is bravely facing her own battle with cancer. But through it all, her resilience, love, and unwavering spirit shine through.

A devoted grandmother of five and a new great-grandmother to identical twin boys, Gloria's legacy is one of strength and devotion. She finds joy in life's simplest pleasures — like watching the birds gather at her feeders. She is deeply loved, and today, we celebrate her remarkable life with gratitude and admiration.

Gloria's advice to her grandchildren:
"Treat people the way you want to be treated yourself."

GLUTEN-FREE APPLE CRISP

With a son who must eat gluten-free, and friends who have celiac disease, I put this together to try it out and it's become a favourite!

INGREDIENTS

7–8 medium-sized apples (peeled)
2 cups GF rolled oats
1 ½ cups brown sugar
1 cup sweetened coconut
2 teaspoons cinnamon
¾ cup soft butter
1 cup chopped pecans

METHOD

In a buttered 9 x13-inch pan, slice the peeled apples and spread out evenly.

Mix the GF rolled oats, sugar, coconut, cinnamon, pecans, and butter together using your hands until it comes together. Take half the mixture and add to the apples. Mix well.

Take the other half and put over the top of the apple mixture. Pat down. Bake at 350°F for about 40 minutes. Serve warm with a scoop of vanilla ice cream.

Featured Grandmother

Sharon Roach

"Nana's kitchen is more than just a place for cooking – it's a warm haven filled with the comforting aromas of her delicious creations."

GINGER CAKE WITH CARAMEL SAUCE

Sharon Roach's recipe

INGREDIENTS

½ cup shortening
½ cup white sugar
1 cup molasses
2 eggs
1 teaspoon cinnamon
1 teaspoon cloves
1 teaspoon ginger
1 teaspoon salt
1 teaspoon baking soda
3 cups sifted flour
¾ cup hot water

METHOD

Put shortening, sugar, molasses, and eggs into mixing bowl and blend. Stir in the hot water. Add the flour, cinnamon, cloves, ginger, salt, and baking soda and mix well. Pour into a greased 9x9 cake pan. Bake at 350°F for 35 minutes.

Caramel Sauce

1 tablespoon cornstarch or flour
½ cup brown sugar
Pinch of salt

Mix the cornstarch/flour, brown sugar and salt together in a saucepan, add cold water to moisten like you would for gravy, stirring until smooth. Add 2 cups boiling water and 2 teaspoons molasses, 1 teaspoon vanilla, and a piece of butter the size of an egg. Cook and stir until thickened. If too thick, add a little more water.

Sharon's advice to her grandchildren: *"It's okay to make mistakes, as long as you learn from them."*

On a blustery winter day in New Waterford, Nova Scotia, stepping into Sharon Roach's kitchen was like being wrapped in a big hug. A bright stove crackled with comforting heat, family gathered close, and the rich, spiced aroma of ginger cake and sauce filled the air. A hot cup of tea and a slice of her famous dessert were all it took to chase away the chill.

Sharon, lovingly known as "Nana" to her family, is more than just a talented baker — she is the heart of her home and a beloved figure in her neighbourhood. In her porch sits a freezer, stocked to the brim with every cookie imaginable. The neighbourhood children know the ritual well; they come to her door, call out "Ding-Dong!" (a playful nod to her broken doorbell) and eagerly request their favourite treat – straight from the freezer.

Despite facing significant health challenges, including chronic back pain, Sharon refuses to let anything keep her from baking. Her kitchen is a haven, rich with family history, where treasured recipe books from her mother and grandmother remain in constant use. With each recipe, she passes down not only the taste of tradition but also the lessons of patience, love, and generosity.

Sharon and her husband, Russell, provide a warm and loving home to their children and grandchildren. Sharon's kindness extends far beyond her baking. She is a giver, a nurturer, and a woman whose love is measured in heaping spoonfuls. No matter the obstacles, her kitchen — and her heart — remain open to all.

CINNAMON APPLE CAKE

INGREDIENTS

5 apples, peeled and diced
1/3 cup white sugar
3 teaspoons cinnamon
2 1/2 cups all-purpose flour
1/2 cup white sugar
4 teaspoons baking powder
2 eggs
1 1/4 cups milk
3 teaspoons vanilla
3 tablespoons melted butter

Topping:
1/2 cup brown sugar
2 1/2 teaspoons cinnamon

METHOD

Set oven to 350°F.

Place the diced apples in a bowl and set aside. In a small bowl, mix the cinnamon and sugar together and pour over the apples. Toss the fruit with the cinnamon sugar mixture until the apples are well coated; set aside.

In a small bowl, mix the flour, sugar, and baking powder.

In a larger bowl, place the next four ingredients and whisk well until eggs are incorporated.

Add the dry ingredients and whisk until smooth and add the apple mixture and fold in until all the apples are nicely mixed in.

Pour into a buttered (or sprayed) 9x13-inch pan. Mix topping ingredients well and sprinkle over the batter.

Drizzle with 1/2 cup melted butter. Bake at 350°F for 45 minutes or until a toothpick/cake tester comes out clean. Remove from oven and place on cooling rack until just warm. Serve while slightly warm with a small scoop vanilla ice cream. So delicious.

Featured Grandmother

Kay Dugas
"My grandmother is an inspiration to many."

Kay's advice to her grandchildren:
"You are my greatest gifts and I love you unconditionally. Always love and take care of each other!"

KAY'S CARROT CAKE

Kay Dugas' recipe

INGREDIENTS

4 eggs, beaten
1 ½ cups vegetable oil
1 ¾ cups white sugar
2 cups carrots, grated
2 cups flour
2 teaspoons baking powder
2 teaspoons baking soda
2 teaspoons cinnamon
1 teaspoon salt
½ cup chopped walnuts
⅔ cup drained crushed pineapple
½ - ¾ cup raisins
½ cup coconut (sweetened or unsweetened)

Icing:

4 ounces softened cream cheese or more
½ cup butter (room temperature)
2 cups icing sugar
1 teaspoon vanilla

Beat the above with electric beater and ice on cooled cake. Garnish with some toasted coconut if desired.

To toast coconut: place 1 cup coconut on a parchment lined cookie sheet and place in a pre-heated 325°F oven for 7-8 minutes. Stir after every couple of minutes until desired colour.

METHOD

With an electric beater, beat the eggs in a large bowl and then add the oil and sugar on low speed. Add the carrots and mix until incorporated.

In a separate bowl, place the dry ingredients and stir. Add them to the egg mixture and mix well with a spoon.

Add the rest of the ingredients and stir just until combined.

Pour into a buttered Bundt pan. Bake at 350°F for 60 minutes.

Just north of Inverness, Nova Scotia, in a cozy kitchen filled with love and laughter, especially when her three children and their families visit from Halifax, Kay Dugas welcomes friends and family with open arms and something delicious on the table. A retired nurse, Kay spent many years caring for others in the operating room at the local hospital, and that same nurturing spirit shines through in everything she does — especially in her cooking and baking.

Kay's granddaughter speaks of her with admiration, describing how her love for food and family has shaped not only cherished memories but also a lifelong passion. The lessons learned in Kay's kitchen extend far beyond measuring cups and mixing bowls. Through baking, she has taught patience, resilience, and the joy of sharing something homemade. Her famous carrot cake is legendary, and I was lucky enough to share a slice with her over a cup of tea. The conversation flowed easily, as it always does with Kay — like catching up with an old friend.

Kay's warmth isn't just in her kitchen but also in her soul. A talented Cape Breton step-dancer, she embodies the energy and spirit of her community. She comes from a long line of MacDonnell tradition bearers. She has been a constant in the organization of the annual Broad Cove Concert which celebrates Cape Breton musical traditions. Her passion for life is contagious, inspiring her granddaughter to follow in her footsteps as she studies to become a nurse at St. Francis Xavier University.

From the aroma of her home-cooked meals to the life lessons passed down through generations, Kay Dugas is the heart of her family. And Kay, I'll be back — ready to enjoy whatever delightful treasures you have waiting.

KINDNESS CAKE

Mary Dickinson is featured later in the book, but I just had to share this recipe. So good and I love the name.

INGREDIENTS

1 cup butter, softened
1 ½ cups granulated sugar
3 eggs
1 tablespoon grated orange rind
3 cups all-purpose flour
1 ½ teaspoons baking soda
½ teaspoon baking powder
½ teaspoon salt
1 ½ cups buttermilk
1 ¼ cups chopped pitted dates
1 cup dried cranberries
1 cup chopped almonds

Icing:
4 tablespoons softened butter
4 cups icing sugar
6 tablespoons orange juice
Zest of one orange

METHOD

Beat the butter with the sugar until fluffy and then beat in the eggs one at a time. Add the orange rind.

In a separate bowl, whisk together the flour, baking soda, baking powder, and salt.

Stir the flour mixture into the butter mixture alternately with buttermilk, making for 3 additions of dry ingredients and 2 of buttermilk. Stir in the dates, cranberries, and almonds until just combined.

Bake in 2 parchment-lined greased loaf pans (8x4-inches) at 350°F for approximately 1 ¼ hours. (If using glass pans reduce heat to 325°F). Bake until a cake tester inserted in the middle comes out clean.

Beat the butter and ½ cup icing sugar and then add the orange juice. Add the remaining icing sugar and zest until the icing is smooth. Spread on cooled cakes.

Yield: 2 cakes – Make a cake to keep and a cake to give!

This cake represents many cultures with their traditional ingredients:
Almonds – from the Jewish Mandelbrot (Mandel – almond / brot – bread).
Dates – eaten to break the fast at end of Ramadan.
Cranberries – from the cuisine of Canada's Indigenous people.

CARROT CHEESECAKE BUNDT CAKE

INGREDIENTS

Wet Ingredients:
2 cups white sugar
1 ½ cups vegetable oil
2 teaspoons vanilla
4 large eggs

Dry Ingredients:
2 ¼ cups all-purpose flour
1 ½ teaspoons baking soda
1 teaspoon baking powder
½ teaspoon salt
¼ teaspoon ginger
¼ teaspoon ground cloves
½ teaspoon nutmeg
2 teaspoons cinnamon
3 cups grated carrots
1 cup chopped pecans

Filling:
1 250-g (8-ounce) package cream cheese (softened)
⅓ cup white sugar
1 teaspoon vanilla
1 large egg

Frosting:
4 ounces softened cream cheese (1/2 package)
3 tablespoons milk
2 cups icing sugar

METHOD

Preheat oven to 350°F. Butter or spray a 12 cup Bundt pan and set aside. (You can also use tube pan or spring form pan). Grate the carrots.

Whisk wet ingredients together until blended and set aside.

Whisk the dry ingredients together until blended and add to wet ingredients. Pour about ¾ of this mixture into the bundt pan and prepare the filling.

Beat filling ingredients well until blended, using a hand mixer. Pour this mixture evenly over the batter in the bundt pan but do not mix. Now spoon or pour the rest of the cake batter evenly over this but do not mix.

Bake at 350°F for 60–65 minutes. The cake will be browned and will slightly pull away from the pan when done. Remove from oven and cool for 10 minutes ONLY before turning upside down and removing the cake onto a wire rack. Cool completely before frosting.

Beat frosting ingredients together until smooth and creamy – it will be runny. Pour the frosting into a plastic bag and snip a corner off the bag. Drizzle all over the cake and sprinkle immediately with chopped pecans.

Featured Grandmother

Tish MacInnis

"Nanny Tishy is the most helpful, thoughtful, and kind nanny."

LOTTIE'S ORANGE CAKE

Tish MacInnis' recipe

INGREDIENTS

1 yellow or golden cake mix
1 package instant lemon pudding
¾ cup vegetable oil
¾ cup orange juice
4 eggs
1 tablespoon lemon extract

Glaze:
½ cup orange juice
⅔ cup white sugar
¼ cup butter

METHOD

Preheat oven to 350°F.

In a large bowl, combine the dry cake mix, the dry pudding, oil, juice, eggs, and lemon extract in a large bowl and mix for 8–10 minutes.

Pour batter into greased or sprayed tube pan/Bundt pan and bake at 350°F for 40–50 minutes.

Remove from oven when toothpick inserted comes out clean. Let cool for 10 minutes and invert onto cake platter.

Combine glaze ingredients in a small saucepan. Boil gently for 2 minutes. Poke a few holes in the cake with a toothpick and pour glaze gently over cake while it is still warm. Serve as is or with a dollop of whipped cream or ice cream.

Tish's advice to her grandchildren: *"When I look into those innocent eyes, I see my past and hope for their future. Their laughter is like medicine for my soul. They are loved beyond anything I could have ever imagined. Each and every one!"*

In the heart of Port Hood, Nova Scotia, Tish MacInnis quietly goes about her days, never seeking attention but always giving her whole heart to the people she loves. A longtime employee at the local Co-op, she keeps things running smoothly in the office with dedication and care.

But it is in her role as a grandmother that Tish truly shines — though she'd never say so herself. Humble and a little shy, she doesn't crave the limelight, but her love, warmth, and generosity deserve to be celebrated.

For Tish, nothing brings more joy than time spent with her grandchildren — Sadie, Hughie, Jack, Lennox, Mae, Joe, and Ben. They speak of her with such love, calling her "Nanny Tishy" and describing her as the most thoughtful and kind person they know. She hosts big family suppers, plans adventures, and ensures there is always something delicious to share at her table.

When it came time to choose a recipe, Tish knew exactly what to submit: a cake from her mother-in-law, Lottie. A simple, delightful treat, this cake holds generations of love and memories in every bite. It's a favourite among her children and grandchildren — a sweet reminder of family traditions and the deep connections that food can bring.

Tish MacInnis may not seek recognition, but her kindness, generosity, and devotion to family speak louder than any spotlight ever could. She is a grandmother beyond measure, and her love is felt in every warm hug, shared meal, and cherished moment together.

Featured Grandmother

Darlene Sutherland

"Nan is the best! She's the heart of our family, always whipping up delicious meals and treats that fill our home with warmth."

Darlene's advice to her grandchildren: *"Always remember the power of kindness – small acts can make the biggest difference in someone's day."*

In the warmth of her family home — the childhood house of her husband, Eldie, — Darlene Sutherland has built a legacy of love, kindness, and tradition. A quiet and unassuming woman, Darlene doesn't seek attention, but her presence is felt in the most meaningful ways. She adores her grandchildren and great-grandchildren, finding immense joy in their laughter and company.

Darlene's love for baking is deeply rooted in family tradition. She treasured her mother-in-law, learning by her side how to make her old-fashioned fruitcake. When her mother-in-law passed, Darlene carried on the tradition, ensuring that each Christmas, a small fruitcake graces the family table — a sweet and heartfelt connection to the past.

Her daughter Angie calls her the heart of their family, always ready with a warm meal or a batch of treats. No one leaves Darlene's home empty-handed; there's always a bag of goodies waiting by the door. But it's not just her family who benefits from her generosity. I have found out that Darlene quietly bakes and cooks for those in the community who are alone, or who are feeling unwell, or perhaps have a birthday or anniversary, ensuring that no one feels forgotten. How beautiful is that? Darlene wouldn't tell you that herself, but what goes around, comes around.

Her kindness is never boastful — it's simply who she is. Through her baking, her love, and her unwavering devotion to family and community, Darlene Sutherland brings light and warmth to all who know her. She may be humble, but to those around her, she is nothing short of extraordinary.

NANNA'S OLD-FASHIONED FRUITCAKE

Darlene Sutherland's recipe

INGREDIENTS

Fruit mixture:
2 pounds dark raisins
1 pound light raisins
1 pound currants
1 cup (250 grams) mixed peel
1 pound pitted dates (chopped)
1 cup red cherries (cut up)
1 cup green cherries (cut up)
Juice and rind of ½ a lemon
Juice and rind of 1 orange
1 cup strawberry jam or apple jelly
1 cup molasses
½ cup dark rum

Dry Ingredients:
6 cups flour
1 teaspoon nutmeg
2 teaspoons cloves
1 teaspoon cinnamon
1 teaspoon baking soda
1 teaspoon baking powder
1 pound butter (room temperature)
2 ¼ cups brown sugar
10 eggs
1 cup coffee

METHOD

In a large bowl, place the fruit mixture ingredients. Mix and cover and let sit overnight.

In the morning, mix the dry ingredients together and toss with the fruit mixture and set aside.

In a large bowl, cream the butter and gradually add sugar until fluffy. Add the 10 eggs in three installments, beating well between additions. Add the coffee and very gradually add the fruit mixture which has been tossed with the dry ingredients.

Pour into desired shaped pans which have been greased and lined with parchment paper. Place the pans in a 300°F oven on middle rack. Add a pan of hot water on lower rack (for steaming). Cover cakes with parchment paper and bake for 2 hours then remove water. Continue baking for 1½ - 2 hours or until a toothpick comes out clean.

Cheesecloth and Rum-soaking: Pour some rum (extra from the rum used in the cake) into a soup bowl and gather up cheesecloth into a ball and gently soak until the cheesecloth is covered but just moist. Wring out if needed, and then wrap each cake, then wrap in parchment paper for storage.

Featured Grandmother

Florence Beaton

"Our grandma is the best and loves to bake with us when we go home."

FLORENCE'S GUMDROP CAKE

Florence Beaton's recipe

INGREDIENTS

8 ounces cream cheese (room temperature)
1 cup salted butter (room temperature)
1 ½ cups white sugar
4 eggs
1 ½ teaspoons almond extract
1 ⅓ cups flour
1 teaspoon baking powder
¾ teaspoon salt
1 ½ cups sugared gumdrops (cut up)
⅔ cup flour

METHOD

Beat the cream cheese and butter until nice and creamy. Add the white sugar and mix well. Add the eggs one at a time, beating after each addition. Add the almond extract and beat well.

Mix the flour, baking powder, and salt in another bowl, and stir into the butter until combined.

Coat the gumdrops with the ⅔ cup flour. Gently fold into the cake batter. Pour into a greased tube pan and bake at 325°F for 1 hour and 25 minutes. Check on it at intervals as it may take a shorter time depending on the stove.

Let cool on rack and use a knife to slide around the edges to help release the cake from the tube pan. Cool until room temperature.

Florence's advice to her grandchildren: *"Get a good education. Life goes by quicker than you think. Make the most of every day so you can look back on a life well lived. No matter where you may end up living, always remember where you came from."*

Down a winding country road in Little Judique, Nova Scotia, Florence Beaton has spent a lifetime nurturing both minds and hearts. A retired teacher, she dedicated her career to guiding six- and seven-year-olds through the joys of reading, writing, and creativity. But her teaching didn't stop at the classroom — her love of learning, music, and tradition has been passed down to her family and community in countless ways.

Florence is also a gifted piano player, known for her generous spirit when it comes to sharing her talent. Whether she's accompanying Cape Breton fiddlers or playing for the St. Peter's church choir in Port Hood, her music brings people together. When she's not at the piano, you might find her around the card table, where she's hard to beat at crib or auction during community games.

Florence and her late husband, Hughie Malcolm, raised two boys and have three granddaughters who are the absolute light of her life. One granddaughter lives in Nova Scotia, while the other two are in Manitoba, but no matter the distance, their connection remains strong — especially through baking.

Her granddaughters Erin and Katie cherish memories of baking alongside her, both at home in Nova Scotia and during her visits to Manitoba. "Grandma always has many baked goods when we visit. Her gumdrop cake at Christmas is a treasured tradition, and her homemade rolls are always waiting for us when we come home. We love our grandma."

STRAWBERRY CHEESECAKE

It was my pleasure to have chef Kelly Gottwald bake on Tunes and Wooden Spoons. *This is the recipe she shared and it is so delicious.*

INGREDIENTS

Crust:
1 ½ cups graham wafer crumbs
¼ cup white sugar
5 tablespoons melted butter

Cream Cheese Filling:
4 packages (250 g each) cream cheese (softened to room temperature)
1 cup white sugar
1 cup sour cream
1 teaspoon vanilla
2 teaspoons lemon juice
3 large eggs (at room temperature)

METHOD

Mix the crumbs and sugar together and then add the melted butter. Press lightly into a 9- or 10-inch springform pan (ungreased) and press a little up the sides. Bake at 350°F for about 10 minutes. Place a large piece of foil wrap on your cooling rack and place your baked crust on the cooling rack while filling is prepared.

In a large bowl, using a hand-held beater or in a stand mixer, beat together the cream cheese and the sugar for about 2 minutes. Add the sour cream, vanilla, and lemon juice and beat for another 2 minutes until light and fluffy. At medium speed, add one egg at a time until the last one is just incorporated and stop mixing. Pour the mixture onto the crust and smooth it out nicely.

BAKING INSTRUCTIONS

Boil a full kettle for the water bath. Wrap the foil around the bottom of the pan and up the sides and place in a larger dish or roast pan and then place on the oven rack. Then pour the kettle of boiling water into the roasting pan or larger dish – the water shouldn't go past the foil that's wrapped around the cheesecake batter.

Bake for about 70 minutes in a 325°F oven. If the middle jiggles a little, that's good – your cheesecake is ready. (150°F on the thermometer is the correct temp for a baked cheesecake.)

Turn the oven off and leave the door ajar for about 1 hour. Remove from the oven and let it come to room temperature. Place plastic wrap over the cheesecake and refrigerate for at least 4 hours or overnight. Slide a knife around the edges of the cheesecake to remove from pan.

Recipe continued on next page

INGREDIENTS

Strawberry Filling

1 pound (about 2 cups) strawberries (washed, hulled, and diced)
¼ cup sugar
1 tablespoon lemon juice
1 tablespoon cornstarch
Water

Whipped Cream

1 cup whipping cream
Vanilla

METHOD

Place the strawberries in a saucepan and sprinkle the sugar on top. Mix the cornstarch with a tiny bit of water and add the lemon juice and then add to the strawberries. Turn heat to medium and stir until it begins to thicken. Remove from heat and let it come to room temperature and then keep in refrigerator until cheesecake has been cooling in the fridge for at least 4 hours. Spread over the top of the cheesecake.

Whip cream and vanilla together until stiff and pipe around the edges of the cheesecake before serving.

Featured Grandmother

Julie Devoe

"My Nan taught my little sister and I how to bake when we were old enough to hold a whisk."

LEMON DREAM CAKE

Julie Devoe's recipe

INGREDIENTS

Cake Mixture:
1 ½ cups sugar
4 eggs (room temperature)
1 cup vegetable oil
2 teaspoons pure vanilla extract
1 cup milk (room temperature)
3 cups flour
1 tablespoon baking powder
½ teaspoon salt

Lemon Filling:
1 ¾ cups sugar
4–5 tablespoons cornstarch
¼ teaspoon salt
4 eggs, separated
1 ¾ cups water
2 tablespoons butter
½ cup lemon juice, freshly squeezed
2 tablespoons flour
1 tablespoon finely shredded lemon peel

Whipped Cream:
1 litre carton whipping cream
⅓ cup icing sugar
¼ cup cream stabilizer *(Optional)
1 teaspoon lemon extract

*Cream stabilizer will allow whipped cream to last longer.

METHOD

Combine sugar, eggs, and vanilla. Beat on medium speed until lightened in colour for about 2 minutes. Add in oil. Whisk dry ingredients together. Add to the egg mixture, alternating with the milk. DO NOT OVERMIX. Grease two 8-inch round baking pans, and line with parchment paper. Add equal amounts of batter to each pan. Place in the pre-heated oven and bake for 33–38 minutes. Check with toothpick for doneness. Cool in pans for 10 minutes before removing.

In a saucepan, combine sugar and cornstarch, flour, and water. Cook and stir constantly until mixture thickens. Add salt, lemon juice, and lemon peel and continue cooking. Stir constantly until blended. Beat egg yolks until smooth. Pour some hot mixture over the beaten egg yolks while whisking constantly. Return mixture to pot and cook for about 4 minutes or until large bubbles break the surface. Remove from heat, add butter, and stir to combine. Let cool before adding to cake.

Mix whipped cream ingredients together until firm peaks form.

Once cake and lemon filling have cooled, assemble the cake. Using the two 8-inch round cakes, slice each cake in two to give you 4 layers. To each layer, add 1 cup lemon filling and 1 cup whipping cream. Decorate the outside of the cake with whipped cream.

The moment you step into Julie's place in Halifax, Nova Scotia, you're met with warmth, hospitality, and the unmistakable scent of something wonderful baking in the oven. Though she calls Halifax home, Julie's Cape Breton roots shine through in her generosity, love of family, and, of course, her passion for baking. A perfectionist in the kitchen, she pours her heart into every creation, sharing her beautifully crafted treats with a devoted following on *Facebook* — a following that wholeheartedly agrees, as do I, that she should have a cookbook of her own!

During my visit, Julie's son Mitchell, his wife, and their two daughters dropped in, offering a glimpse into just how much Nan and her husband, James, cherish their family. Their home is not just a gathering place — it's a haven for their grandchildren, complete with a perfectly organized playroom, stocked with anything a little one could need for a visit or a sleepover.

But the heart of the home is Julie's kitchen, where every possible baking tool is at her fingertips. While one cake was already baked and assembled, another was in the works — because for Julie, everything has to be just right.

Her granddaughters treasure every moment spent baking with her. "She has taught us since we could hold a whisk. She lets us do every part of it, making sure it's always fun." But more than her skill in the kitchen, they admire her heart of gold. "We love you, Nan!"

Julie's advice to her grandchildren: *"Make with love and it will always feed the heart."*

FROZEN LEMON PARFAIT WITH RASPBERRY COULIS

Here in my hometown of Port Hood, the Clove Hitch Bar and Bistro had a dessert similar to this recipe. I ordered it every time I went there for supper so decided I would try and make my own version. If you love lemon, this is for you.

Reminders before beginning:
Have eggs at room temperature. If you are making the garnishes (compote and curd), you'll need 9 eggs in total. Zest your lemons before juicing (the juice from 3 lemons should give you enough to use in the parfait AND the lemon curd). Microwave each lemon for 10 seconds before juicing to get more juice. Line the bottom and sides of an 8-inch springform pan.

INGREDIENTS

Parfait:
¾ cup white sugar
2 ½ tablespoons cornstarch
5 eggs
⅔ cup lemon juice (about 3 lemons)

Meringue:
¼ cup white sugar
2 egg whites (save the egg yolks if you are making the lemon curd garnish below)

METHOD

In a saucepan, combine the sugar and cornstarch until blended. Add the eggs and whisk all together. Add the lemon juice and stir well. Over medium-low heat, bring the mixture to a boil until thickened (about 3-4 minutes). Remove from heat and cover with plastic wrap and place in refrigerator for 20 minutes. Remove from the fridge and set in some cold water in the sink while you prepare the meringue.

Beat the egg whites with the sugar until stiff peaks form. When the lemon parfait has cooled, fold in the meringue. Pour into the 8-inch prepared springform pan and sprinkle with lemon zest. Cover with foil and place in the freezer for at least 6 hours before serving.

For serving: Serve as is or add a couple of spoonfuls of cooled raspberry compote (and a couple of fresh raspberries) and a dollop of lemon curd as per recipe below, which makes about 1 cup. Adds such a nice garnish.

INGREDIENTS

Lemon Curd:

4 tablespoons butter (cut into smaller pieces and set aside)
1 large egg and 3 large egg yolks
½ cup sugar
Zest and juice of 1 lemon (gives you anywhere from 1 teaspoon to 1 tablespoon zest) and about a ¼ cup of juice

Raspberry Coulis:

2 cups raspberries
¼ cup white sugar
3 tablespoons water
1 ½ teaspoons cornstarch that has been dissolved in a tiny bit of water.

METHOD

Prep all the ingredients before cooking.

In a saucepan, whisk together the whole egg, the egg yolks, sugar, lemon zest, and lemon juice. Bring to a simmer over medium-low heat, whisking constantly. Cook until mixture is thickened, about 2 ½ to 3 minutes. Remove from heat. Add in the butter – whisking a little piece at a time – and don't add the next piece until the first has melted into the hot lemon. Press plastic wrap directly onto the surface of the lemon curd and refrigerate until cold. Yield of lemon curd is 1 cup. So lemony and delicious.

Mix the raspberry coulis ingredients together in a saucepan and simmer for about 6 minutes, then add cornstarch.

Mix well and leave on heat for about 1 minute. Cover surface with plastic wrap and refrigerate.

Featured Grandmother

Barbara Blizzard

"We love her beyond measure."

UNBELIEVABLE CHOCOLATE CAKE

Barbara Blizzard's recipe

INGREDIENTS

½ cup melted butter
2 cups white sugar
2 eggs
1 teaspoon vanilla
2 cups flour
1 teaspoon baking powder
2 teaspoons baking soda
¾ cup cocoa
Pinch of salt
1 cup milk
1 cup boiling water

METHOD

Mix in any order but add the boiling water last. This makes a very thin batter. Will make a 9x13-inch cake or 2 small cakes. Bake at 350°F for 35–40 minutes. If using a tube pan, will need to add cooking time. Check for doneness. This makes a dense cake and is so delicious!

Barbara's advice to her grandchildren: *"My grandkids said they always felt lots of love from Nanny and there was always dessert at Nan's house. Someday, when they compare notes, they may each even say, 'Nanny told me I was her favourite!'"*

From the moment Barbara Blizzard greeted us at her door in Fredericton, New Brunswick, she embodied the very spirit of this book — "Come In" — and, true to tradition, she put the kettle on. Settling into her cozy living room, we chatted like old friends, surrounded by cherished photos and memories from days gone by.

Barbara spoke lovingly of her late husband, Earle, the love of her life and her constant companion for 56 years. She misses him deeply, but she shared how *Tunes and Wooden Spoons* became a source of comfort during her hardest days, offering a weekly connection with familiar faces and a sense of community, even from afar. She looked forward to Sundays — whether baking along, watching, or simply enjoying the chatter finding solace in the warmth of shared traditions.

Though her son lives in Saint John, NB, and her daughter in Ontario, they remain close through phone calls, FaceTime, and visits. And when her granddaughter, Claire, called during our visit, it was clear just how much love surrounds Barbara, even across the miles.

Her granddaughter's nomination speaks volumes: *"Nanny Blizzard has been through a tough few years, but her love for family has never wavered. Her baking may have slowed down, but when we visit, there are always fresh biscuits and chocolate cake waiting. She has created so many beautiful memories and traditions for us. We love her beyond measure."*

Barbara, you made a lasting impression on me, and I promise—I'll be back for a visit.

APPLE AND CREAM CHEESE TORTE

Received this from a follower of Tunes and Wooden Spoons *– thank you Elizabeth Wallace.*

INGREDIENTS

Base:
½ cup butter softened
⅓ cup sugar
1 cup flour
⅓ cup raspberry jam

Filling:
8-ounce package cream cheese
¼ cup sugar
1 egg
1 teaspoon vanilla

Topping:
3 cups apples, peeled (thinly sliced)
⅓ cup sugar
½ teaspoon cinnamon
½ cup sliced almonds

METHOD

Cream butter and sugar and blend in flour and press into bottom and up the side of springform pan. Spread with jam.

Beat filling ingredients together and pour over jam layer.

Toss sliced apples in sugar mixed with cinnamon. Arrange on top of base. Sprinkle with sliced almonds. Bake at 450°F for 10 minutes and reduce heat to 400°F and bake for a further 25-30 minutes. Let cool slightly before removing rim.

Featured Grandmother

Malvina Robichaud Daneault

"My mother is 94 and she is still the most wonderful cook ever. I use all her recipes and always have. She is the best."

BELGIAN CAKE

Malvina Robichaud Daneault's recipe

INGREDIENTS

¾ cup butter (room temperature)
2 cups white sugar
3 eggs
3 cups all-purpose flour
1 teaspoon cream of tartar
1 teaspoon baking soda
1 cup milk
1 teaspoon vanilla

Cream Cheese Frosting:
½ cup soft butter
8-ounce package of cream cheese (room temperature)
1 teaspoon vanilla
4 cups icing sugar

METHOD

Cream the butter and add in the white sugar and mix well. Add in the eggs one at a time.

Mix dry ingredients together. Mix the milk and vanilla together. Add the dry ingredients alternately with the milk and vanilla, beginning and ending with the dry ingredients.

Pour into a well-greased tube pan and bake at 350°F for 1 hour or until the toothpick comes out clean.

Beat frosting ingredients with electric beater and spread over cooled cake.

In the beautiful fishing town of Shippagan, New Brunswick, where Acadian pride runs deep, lives a remarkable woman named Malvina Robichaud Daneault. At 94 years young, Malvina's warmth, grace, and energy defy her years. Though she speaks almost exclusively French, communication was never a barrier — because in Malvina's home, food is its own language. With the kind assistance of her daughter Doris, who translated our conversation, we shared stories, laughter, and, of course, something sweet from her kitchen.

Malvina's life has been one of resilience and love. Widowed young, she raised a large family of eight children and later found happiness again, marrying Louis. Their home proudly displays countless photos of their children, grandchildren, and great-grandchildren — a testament to the love and memories they've built together, many of which were created around the family table.

For our visit, Malvina chose to bake a cake passed down from her mother-in-law, a recipe treasured through generations. We sat together in her immaculate home, savouring a slice of history, a hot cup of tea, and conversation that transcended words. She also shared a crumb cake recipe from her late mother's recipe collection, a true gift of tradition.

Malvina is more than a talented baker — she is a pillar of her family, a proud Acadian, and a woman whose kindness leaves a lasting impression. Merci, Malvina, merci, may we meet again.

Malvina's advice to her grandchildren:
"Apprendre les deux langues. Aller étudier pour avoir une bonne view. Prendre soins déux-autres. (Learn both languages, French and English. Go and study so you have something with which to make a living and have a good life. Take care of yourselves.)"

BREADS, MUFFINS, AND MORE

JOELLA'S BAGELS

Joella Foulds is the co-founder of Cape Breton's Celtic Colours International Festival. She joined me on Tunes and Wooden Spoons Facebook *livestream show and shared how she makes her delicious bagels.*

INGREDIENTS

1 ½ cups warm water
2 ¾ teaspoons instant or active dry yeast
1 tablespoon brown sugar
2 teaspoons salt
4 cups bread flour
One egg white

For boiling:
2 quarts water
¼ cup honey

METHOD

Whisk the warm water and yeast together in a bowl and let stand 5 minutes. Pour into a large bowl or in your stand mixer.

Whisk in brown sugar and salt.

Add flour, 1 cup at a time.

Turn out onto floured surface and knead for 4–5 minutes.

Lightly grease a large bowl with olive oil. Coat all sides of the dough and cover with plastic wrap or a dish towel and allow to rise at room temperature for 60–90 minutes or until double in bulk.

Line two baking sheets (or one large one) with parchment paper and preheat oven to 425°F.

Prepare egg wash: whisk one egg white with 1 tablespoon water and set aside.

Punch down the risen dough and cut into 8 equal pieces. Shape each piece into a ball. Make a hole in each ball with your thumb. Stretch the hole slightly to form a bagel shape. Place bagels on the baking sheets and rest for a few minutes while you prepare the water bath.

Place the water in a Dutch oven and whisk in the honey. Bring to a boil.

Drop in 2–3 bagels at a time, allowing enough room for them to move around freely. Cook 1 minute on each side. Remove from the water, rest briefly on a towel and brush with egg wash on top and sides. Sprinkle with desired toppings. Place bagels on baking sheet. Bake for 20–25 minutes, until golden brown.

Remove from oven, cool on baking sheet for 20 minutes and then transfer to cooling rack.

Everything Bagel Seasoning

2 tablespoons dried garlic flakes (or powder)
2 ½ tablespoons dried onion flakes
1 ½ tablespoons white sesame seeds
1 tablespoon poppy seeds
1 tablespoon black sesame seeds (optional)
Heaping ½ tablespoon sea salt

Mix until thoroughly combined.

Featured Grandmother

Donna Peterson

"I was 11 when she first introduced me to baking homemade bread."

NANA HILLMAN'S BROWN BREAD/ROLLS

Donna Peterson's recipe

INGREDIENTS

¾ cup white sugar
Handful of rolled oats (about ½ cup)
1 egg (beaten)
¾ cup fancy molasses
2 or 3 shakes of salt (about 1 teaspoon)
¾ cup shortening
4 cups boiling water
2 heaping tablespoons of quick-rise yeast
8 cups all-purpose flour (or 7 cups all-purpose plus 1 cup whole wheat flour)

METHOD

In a large bread-making bowl, mix together the sugar, rolled oats, and egg. Stir well to combine. Stir in molasses and salt. Beat in shortening with a whisk. Add boiling water one cup at a time and stir. Let cool before adding yeast. (Tip: Put cold water in the kitchen sink and place bowl in water to cool down mixture to lukewarm – no more than 110 degrees.) Add yeast, stir, and let sit till yeast foams (about 10 minutes). Add flour 1 cup at a time and mix well.

Put dough out on a floured surface and knead, adding a slight amount of extra flour to take away stickiness. The secret to good bread is KNEAD, KNEAD, KNEAD. After kneading for approximately 10 minutes, let dough sit for 10–15 minutes. Knead once again for 5–8 minutes before placing dough in greased bowl. Cover bowl with tea towel and set on top of stove to double in size 1 hour (Tip: Preheat oven to 350°F and then turn off for residual heat to rise to stove top to help proof dough.) After dough has risen, poke the dough to deflate. This recipe will make 4–5 loaves, depending on pan size.

Divide dough into 8–10 equal size pieces. Work one piece of dough, tucking in and under and then smack the top of dough before shaping and placing in on half of greased loaf pan. Repeat for other end of loaf pan. After all pans are full, use a fork and poke 4 indents into each loaf before letting loaves rise and then cover until double in size.

Bake in a 350°F oven till crust is golden brown and sounds hollow when tapped, approximately 25–30 minutes. If using whole wheat, bake in a 375°F oven for 25–30 minutes.

If making the recipe into buns, depending on size of buns, this batch should make about 30 buns. Bake buns for 20 minutes.

Remove loaves to wire rack and brush tops with butter and allow to cool.

From the moment Donna Peterson opened her door at her Hartland, NB, home, she left a lasting impression. Gracefully dressed, adorned with a pearl necklace and matching earrings, and with every hair perfectly in place, she carried herself with elegance and warmth.

A proud mother of one son, Kevin, and mother-in-law to Stephanie, she has one beloved grandson, Tristan. Donna's love for her family shines through in every word she speaks. She and her late husband, Carl, were dedicated pillars of their community and church, giving generously of their time and talents.

From teaching Sunday School, to leading choirs, she did it all. Music has always been a part of Donna's life. An amazing pianist, she has also led numerous handbell choirs over the years, guiding groups of senior ladies, young married couples, and even a small girls' choir. When she sat down at the piano during our visit, she played a couple of beautiful Christian hymns — though she worried it wouldn't be good enough for us. It was more than enough; it was absolutely lovely.

Her cozy senior unit backs onto Hartland's Community Playground next to the arena, where children gather to play and have fun. Right by her back door sits a freezer, always stocked with treats, making her a neighbourhood legend. The local kids know her well — she's affectionately called the "Popsicle Lady," and the moment that door opens, they come running with bright smiles.

But Donna's hospitality doesn't stop at popsicles. Her brown bread and rolls were nothing short of delicious, warm and comforting in every bite. Her table was set with meticulous care — fine cups and saucers, a proper tea service that would have surely met the Queen of England's approval.

From the first moment to the last, Donna welcomed us as if we were lifelong friends. Her grace, kindness, and generosity made our visit truly special — a memory to be treasured.

Donna's advice to her grandchild: *"Believe in yourself as much as I believe in you. Be Bold, Be You, Be Kind, Be Truthful, Be Friendly. Never forget that Tristan, I LOVE YOU."*

ENGLISH MUFFINS

INGREDIENTS

1 ¼ cups warm water
1 tablespoon white sugar
1 teaspoon instant dry yeast
2 tablespoons melted butter
2 ¾ cups all-purpose flour
1 teaspoon salt
Cornmeal (for coating)

METHOD

Put the warm water, sugar, and yeast in a medium-sized glass bowl, stir, and let it sit for 10 minutes.

Place in a larger bowl (or in stand-mixer bowl) and add the melted butter and salt. Mix well and add the flour a cup at a time until all added. If using a stand mixer, mix until dough comes away from the sides of the bowl and put on high for about 2 minutes. If mixing by hand, place dough on work surface and knead for about 5 minutes.

Place the kneaded dough in an oiled bowl, cover with plastic wrap or tea towel, and place in a cold oven with the oven light turned on. Also, boil the kettle and put a pot of the boiled water into the oven and let the dough rise until doubled in bulk – 1 hour. Place the dough on a floured surface and knead just a few times and then cut the dough into 10 equal pieces (each piece should weigh about 2.5 ounces approximately). Roll each piece into a ball.

Have some cornmeal in a bowl and coat all sides of each ball of dough and place on a parchment-lined cookie sheet. Flatten each roll down until it's about ½ inch thick. Cover all with a tea towel and set aside for about 20 minutes.

Turn your skillet* to 325°F and lightly butter the surface. Place about 3–4 rolls in the skillet and place cover on top and set the timer for 10 minutes. Each muffin will rise while cooking but resist the urge to flatten down. When 10 minutes is up, flip each muffin, replace the cover, and set your timer for 5 minutes. Transfer to your cooling rack and continue baking the rest in the same fashion. Do not test the cooked muffins until they are completely at room temperature. Don't add any more butter in between batches.

When it's time to test your muffin, it is best to use a fork to pierce all the way around the muffin and then open up the muffin. Great toasted as well.

* I use a Teflon-coated electric griddle that has a glass cover. Best thing ever!!

Featured Grandmother

Gloria Walsh

"My Grammie bakes as much as she is able, and it makes her so happy to be able to still bake for us."

Gloria's advice to her grandchildren:
"Treat people the way you want to be treated."

GLORIOUS RAISIN BREAD

Gloria Walsh's recipe

INGREDIENTS

Milk mixture:

1 ½ cups milk
¾ cup water
½ cup brown sugar
¼ cup molasses
1 large tablespoon shortening
1 teaspoon butter
¼ teaspoon salt
1 pound of sticky raisins (or raisins of choice)

Yeast:

¾ cup lukewarm water (110°F)
1 teaspoon sugar
4 ½ teaspoons active dry yeast

1 beaten egg
1 ½ teaspoons cinnamon
7 cups of flour

METHOD

Bring milk mixture just to the boil and bring to lukewarm. (No more than 110°F.)

Place the raisins in a bowl, cover with hot water, and let them sit while the yeast is rising. Drain and set aside. This will plump up the raisins.

Stir sugar into water until dissolved and add the yeast. Stir slightly and let stand for 15–20 minutes.

To the lukewarm milk mixture, add the egg and cinnamon. Mix gently and then add the yeast mixture. Stir well and add the plumped raisins.

Add the flour a cup at a time while stirring with a wooden spoon or a stand mixer. Continue until you have roughly 1 cup left to sprinkle on the work surface. Remove dough from bowl and knead well until flour is incorporated.

Place dough into an oiled dish and let rise until doubled – about 2 hours. Punch down and divide the dough in half. Form dough into 2 loaves and place in greased loaf pans. Let rise again for about 1 ½ hours.

Preheat the oven to 350°F and bake for 40–45 minutes until a rich brown colour (or internal temperature of 190°F). Remove from pans onto a cooling rack and brush with butter.

From the moment Margie and I arrived at Gloria Walsh's home in Prince Edward Island, we were greeted with one of the biggest, brightest smiles imaginable (complete with some nice red lipstick too). Her smile never faded throughout our visit, a true reflection of the warmth and kindness that defines her.

Gloria had a spread on the table that was simply irresistible. Among the delicious offerings was her famous Raisin Brown Bread — a cherished family favourite. With a pat of butter and a steaming cup of tea, every bite was pure comfort. But the feast didn't end there. She also treated us to her delectable meatballs with a rich, flavourful dipping sauce — so good that she generously shared the recipe with us.

A mother to five children and a dedicated nurse for many years, Gloria decided it was time to retire in 2019. Though health challenges have tried to slow her down, they haven't dampened her spirit. She's turned to baking and cooking as a source of comfort and therapy, pouring her heart into the kitchen. More than anything, she cherishes time spent with her grandchildren Aidan, Nate, and Simon, and baking for them – they are the true light of her life.

Through it all, her greatest supporter has been her husband, Elmer, always by her side, encouraging her every step of the way. Apparently between this husband and wife, he holds the trophy for the best biscuits, and he wears that badge of honour with pride. Gloria's gentle nature, humility, and unwavering kindness make her a truly special person — one who embraces each day with gratitude and grace.

Before we left, I couldn't help but think, I'll definitely be back for another visit! Perhaps I'll even challenge Elmer to a biscuit bake-off!

NAT'S ONE-HOUR BREAD

Natalie MacMaster, fiddler, wife of Donnell Leahy, and mother of seven beautiful children who are all very musical. I am proud to call Natalie my niece. She shared this quick bread recipe!

INGREDIENTS

5 ¼ cups flour
¼ cup white sugar
½ tablespoon salt
1 ½ tablespoons (heaping) instant yeast
1 ½ tablespoons oil
2 cups hot tap water

METHOD

Mix dry ingredients using a stand mixer with hook attachment.

Add oil and hot water.

Mix on medium for 1 minute. Check the dough – it should be slightly wet. Usually, 2 more tablespoons of hot water are added at this point. Up to a ¼ cup of water can be added if the dough is still dry.

Mix on high for 5 minutes (timed). When done, take your dough out and cut it in half. Shape into oval or circular loaves and place on parchment lined cookie sheet (with a little cooking spray on it). Cover with a tea towel and set in warm spot to rise for 25 minutes.

Take a sharp knife and score 3 diagonal cuts and a cross in your circular loaf. Spray a light mist of water over top to make a crispier crust.

Set in 350°F pre-heated oven for 25 minutes. Remove from oven and place on cooling rack.

Featured Grandmother

Gayle MacDonald

"She is the heart and soul of our family's kitchen."

MARY JESSIE'S WHITE BREAD

Gayle MacDonald's recipe

INGREDIENTS

1 cup lukewarm water
1 teaspoon white sugar
2 teaspoons active dry yeast
2 cups milk
6 cups lukewarm water
¼ cup shortening
2 tablespoons salt
¼ cup white sugar
18 cups white flour (pre-measured)

METHOD

In a small bowl, combine the lukewarm water, white sugar, and yeast. Stir gently and let sit for about 10 minutes until it becomes foamy. In a saucepan on medium heat, warm the milk with the lukewarm water. Add shortening, salt, and ¼ cup of white sugar. Stir until the shortening is fully dissolved. Do not let it boil or get too hot, as this can kill the yeast.

In a very large mixing bowl, pour in the warm milk mixture and make sure it is no warmer than 110°F. Whisk in the yeast mixture. Gradually add 2 cups of flour at a time, whisking as much air into the dough as possible in the early stages. As the dough thickens, switch to using your hands. Continue adding flour, 2 cups at a time, until the dough reaches the right consistency. For this batch, 17 ½ cups of flour were incorporated, with the final ½ cup used for flouring the surface.

Turn the dough onto a floured surface and knead for 5 minutes until it becomes elastic and bounces back when pressed (it should not be sticky). Cover the dough with plastic wrap and let it rest for 5 minutes. Knead once more before transferring it to a greased container. Cover with plastic wrap and a blanket or towel to keep it warm.

First Rise:
Let the dough rise for 30 minutes. Punch it down, then allow it to rise again for 1 ½ to 2 hours until it triples in size. Grease loaf pans (5¾ inch x 5¾ inch x 2¾ inch) generously with shortening. Shape the dough into loaves and place them in the prepared pans. Cover and let rise for another 1 ½ hours.

Preheat the oven to 400°F. Bake for approximately 30–40 minutes, or until the crust is a deep golden brown. Immediately after removing from the oven, butter the tops of the loaves. Listen for the crackling sound, a sign of a perfect loaf! Transfer the loaves onto a cooling rack and allow them to cool before slicing. This recipe produces six large double loaves. Enjoy Mary Jessie's legendary homemade white bread!

Mary Jessie, Gayle's late mother-in-law.

Gayle's advice to her grandchildren:
"Do small things with a big heart."

Gayle MacDonald's home is her castle in Mabou Harbour, Nova Scotia, but I met up with her for our visit at her daughter Tracey's home in Port Hawkesbury. It was a heartwarming experience to be with this humble and kind Grandma.

For years, Gayle has been renowned for her delicate, aromatic loaves of bread, and true to her reputation, six feather-light loaves awaited us upon arrival. Humble and gracious, Gayle puts family above all else, a sentiment beautifully expressed by her grandson Dylan in his nomination: "Grandma crafts meals that are both comforting and unforgettable. One of my favourite childhood memories is when she taught me to make her famous bread for my Grade 4 history fair project. It wasn't just about following a recipe — it was a bonding experience, full of laughter and learning."

Gayle's cooking is legendary in her family. Whether it's her mouthwatering spareribs, irresistible homemade jams and jellies, or her perfectly soft bread and rolls, every dish carries the warmth of tradition and love. For over 52 years, she has ensured her husband, Howie, is well-fed — so much so that he refuses to eat store-bought bread!

Her culinary spirit extends to her children and grandchildren, for whom she is always willing to try new recipes. Her meals have been the backdrop to a childhood filled with happiness, fostering a deep appreciation for home-cooked food. Gayle's dedication to her family through her cooking is a true testament to the love and care she pours into every dish, leaving a lasting legacy of warmth, tradition, and, of course, the best bread in Mabou Harbour and beyond.

OLIEBOLLEN

Toosje (Van Berkel) Van de Sande made the recipe on my Tunes and Wooden Spoons Facebook *livestream show. This is a recipe loved by the Dutch people and is made especially at New Year's.*

INGREDIENTS

3 ¼ cups flour
4 ½ teaspoons fast-rising yeast
1 cup milk
¼ cup butter
⅓ cup sugar
1 teaspoon salt
1 teaspoon vanilla
3 eggs
Cooking oil
Icing sugar

METHOD

Combine flour and yeast. Heat milk, butter, sugar, and salt. Cool and add vanilla. Beat eggs well and add to cooled milk. Add liquids to dry ingredients and mix well. Cover and let rise until doubled in size – about 1 hour.

Heat cooking oil to 375°F. Drop by teaspoonfuls into hot fat and fry until golden brown. Drain on paper towel. Serve hot sprinkled with icing sugar.

Make about 36.

SOFT 12-GRAIN BREAD

I make this often. A healthy alternative to white bread.

INGREDIENTS

- ½ cup 12-grain cereal (or fewer grains – 5 or 7)
- 1 ¾ cups boiling water
- 2 ¼ teaspoons active dry yeast (1 pkg.)
- 3 tablespoons packed light or dark brown sugar
- 3 tablespoons salted butter
- 3 ⅓ cups all-purpose flour
- ¼ cup flax seeds (or seed or nut of choice)

METHOD

Step 1: Place the cereal and the boiling water into a heatproof bowl and stir and let it stand for about 20–25 minutes. The thermometer should read no more than 110°F.

Step 2: After the cereal/boiling water has cooled to lukewarm (110°F), add the brown sugar and stir until the sugar is dissolved, then add the yeast and stir well. Let stand for about 20 minutes and then stir.

Step 3: Add the butter and 1 cup of flour and stir by hand or in stand mixer (with beater attachment) on low for about 30 seconds. Add another cup of flour. Beat (or knead) on low and then medium speed until relatively incorporated.

Step 4: Switch to dough hook and add all the remaining flour and the flax seeds and keep on high for about 2 minutes (or knead for about 5 minutes). Make sure you lock your mixer.

The dough should be coming away from the sides of the bowl by now, so if kneading, remove to your counter dusted with some flour and continue to knead. If using a stand mixer, let it knead on medium speed for about 5 minutes.

Step 5: Place in an oiled bowl making sure all sides are oiled. Cover with plastic wrap and place in the oven where there are no drafts. (Place a pot of boiling water in the oven to encourage warmth.) Let rise for 1 hour and 45 minutes

Step 6: Lay dough on work surface and either:

Cut in two and place each one in a parchment-lined (and sprayed) 8.5x4.5-loaf pan; OR cut in two and make 2 round dough balls. Prepare two round, 8-inch cake pans by lining the bottom with parchment and spraying the sides of the pans. Place each ball in the centre of the pan.

Step 7: Place the bread in the oven again with a pot of boiling water and let rise for 1 hour.

Step 8: Remove from the oven and set aside and pre-heat the oven to 350°F. Bake for 40 minutes.

Step 9: Once baked, remove from the pan right away and place on cooling rack and brush with butter.

Featured Grandmother

Rita Landry

"A lady with a whole lot of baking experience!"

The Acadian village of Pomquet, Nova Scotia, is a picturesque, close-knit community where everyone works together to keep things running smoothly. One of its most cherished residents is Rita Landry, a remarkably young-at-heart 101-year-old who has witnessed the village's growth and prosperity over the decades.

Rita keeps busy knitting beautiful dishcloths — one of which she generously gifted me — playing cards, saying her Rosary, or heading to the pantry to bake. Whether whipping up her famous rolls or assisting her granddaughter Debbie in a baking marathon, Rita's kitchen is always warm and welcoming. Among her many specialties, she is particularly known for her pastry skills, especially in crafting traditional pork pies — an East Coast delight made with a shortbread-like crust, a filling of dates, and a dollop of maple icing.

When Rita bakes, she works with whatever ingredients she has on hand, substituting, when necessary, without missing a beat. The results are always delicious, a testament to her experience and intuition in the kitchen. Her cooking prowess extends beyond her home — years ago, she welcomed teachers who came to work at Pomquet's French school, undoubtedly ensuring they were well-fed during their stay.

Her warm kitchen is anchored by a wood stove, its heat unmatched in comfort. Sitting at her table with a hot cup of tea was a true pleasure, and her rolls — soft, flavorful, and undeniably the best I've ever tasted — left a lasting impression. I didn't leave empty-handed either, as she kindly sent me off with two dozen.

Rita embodies the beauty of aging gracefully, embracing each day with gratitude and joy. She is a treasure in every sense of the word, and I look forward to visiting her again when the book comes out.

RITA'S ROLLS

Rita Landry's recipe

INGREDIENTS

4 cups lukewarm water
2 eggs
8 tablespoons white sugar
3 tablespoons quick-rise yeast
1 teaspoon salt
1 cup vegetable oil
10–11 cups flour

METHOD

Beat eggs, add sugar, oil, and add lukewarm water. Add yeast and salt. Add 2–3 cups of flour at a time. Keep working in the rest of the flour. Ten cups of flour should be enough but depending on the flour – if the dough is still sticky, you may need to add more. Knead well together and form into a ball. Let sit for 15 minutes and knead again. Let rise until doubled in size (about 1 ½ hours).

Form into rolls and let rise again until doubled in size (about 1 hour). Bake at 350°F, for 15-20 minutes and, if desired, brush with butter.

Rita's advice to her grandchildren:
"Don't be afraid to substitute."

Featured Grandmother

Heather Hayne is now happily retired, with her husband, Derek, in the beautiful town of Antigonish, having moved there after living the majority of her life in Country Harbour, Guysborough County, Nova Scotia.

For years, Heather ran a rooming house for men who worked at a nearby plant. At times, there were up to 12 men rooming in the lower level of their home. Can you even imagine the number of breakfasts, lunches, and suppers this lady had to make for all these hungry working men?

She hasn't lost that baking love — despite having cooked her heart out for her roomers, she also had her two sons Anil and Aaro to cater to. Now, her grandsons Myers and Jack eagerly await her homemade treats.

Jack, a member of the Junior A team Amherst Ramblers, also gets called up to play for the Moncton Wildcats of the Major Junior League, and Heather and Derek are his proudest fans.

Meanwhile, Myers attends the University of New Brunswick and has played soccer for the university. He and his roommates are always thrilled when Nanny sends him back with a batch of homemade goodies. Granddaughters Eva and Carley absolutely love Nanny's goodies as well. Eva is a student at St. Francis Xavier University and Carley is in Grade 11. These four grandchildren can't say enough about Nanny's goodies!

One of Heather's most treasured possessions is a set of old, black, large loaf pans that once belonged to her mother. These well-seasoned pans, black as coal from years of use in an old wood stove, are a testament to a lifetime of baking tradition. Even in retirement, Heather can't stop baking — there's always something fresh for tea when friends drop by.

I loved making her amazing banana bread with her and then sharing a hot cup of tea to go along with it. Next time I'm nearby, I'll be sure to stop in to see what's cooking!

BANANA BREAD

Heather Hayne's recipe

INGREDIENTS

½ cup margarine
1 ½ cups white sugar
2 eggs
4 bananas, mashed
2 cups flour
1 teaspoon baking powder
½ teaspoon salt
½ cup milk
1 teaspoon vanilla
½ teaspoon baking soda

METHOD

Cream margarine, sugar, and eggs. Add bananas, flour, baking powder, salt, vanilla, and soda. Add the milk last. Line the pan(s) with parchment paper. Bake at 300°F for 1 hour and 15 minutes. Makes 1 large loaf (12x4.5) or 2 small ones.

Heather's advice to her grandchildren: *Always be kind and treat others the way you want to be treated."*

Featured Grandmother

Jessie MacDonald

"She is a huge part of the community and everyone who knows her loves her."

When I received the nomination for Jessie MacDonald, my first thought was, *where in the world is Glenelg, Nova Scotia?* One thing this journey has shown me is that there are some absolutely charming country roads and communities in our Maritime provinces and we need to explore where we live. That's how I found Jessie: this rural road led me to this charming little settlement in Guysborough County, where Jessie has spent most of her 87 years. When I visited with her, she was visiting her daughter's home just down the road from her home, and there she sat — surrounded by a gathering of children, grandchildren, and great-grandchildren. Jessie beamed with quiet joy — because for her, love lives in the presence of family.

Jessie had seven children and now delights in her 14 grandchildren and ten great-grandchildren — with one more on the way. She treasures them all. In an effort to make her really smile for daughter Margie, who was taking the pictures, I prompted this camera-shy grandmother; "Do you remember the first time you kissed your husband?" Her laughter lit up the room and throwing her head back, she laughed heartily before answering, "Yes, I do!" Now widowed, she spoke of her husband with warmth and fondness.

She was nominated by her daughter-in-law Denise who says, "Jessie is the heart of her family. In the 35 years I've known her, she has done everything for us — from cooking Sunday dinners to serving up holiday feasts. Waking up in her home meant the scent of rising rolls, cooling cookies, and pies in the oven. No one ever left hungry — she made sure of that."

A gentle soul, Jessie takes pride in passing down generations-old recipes, including her famous soft sandwich buns and a cherished cinnamon dressing from her grandmother. In her presence, I felt at home — she embodies everything we crave in a grandmother: humility, kindness, and love. I simply adore her.

SANDWICH BUNS

Jessie MacDonald's recipe

INGREDIENTS

4 cups warm water
6 ¾ teaspoons quick-rising yeast
¾ cup white sugar
3 teaspoons salt
¼ cup oil
2 beaten eggs
About 8 cups flour

METHOD

Combine the water, yeast, sugar, salt, oil, and beaten eggs and then add the flour, 2 cups at a time, leaving about ½ cup flour to spread on the counter.

Knead the dough for at least 10 minutes until all the flour is absorbed. Place the dough in a greased bowl and let rise until doubled in bulk (about 1 ½ hours).

Roll into hamburger-shaped balls and place on a greased or parchment-lined cookie sheet. Let rise for 45-60 minutes.

Bake at 350°F for approximately 18-20 minutes until golden brown. Jessie likes to tap on the top of the roll and if the sound is hollow, the buns are done.

Remove from pan and place on a cooling rack and brush with butter. Makes about 24 large hamburger-sized buns.

Jessie's advice to her grandchildren:
My wish is for all my grandchildren to be healthy, happy, and enjoy every minute of your lives. Time goes by so quickly. I've enjoyed watching you grow and become thoughtful, caring, and kind individuals. I cherish each and every one of you."

Featured Grandmother

Donna MacIver

"My grandmother has been a constant in my life. It's not just about the food – it's about the love and care she puts into everything she makes."

OLD-FASHIONED DATE-FILLED OATCAKES

Donna MacIver's recipe

INGREDIENTS

Date Filling:
1 cup chopped dates
⅔ cup water
½ cup sugar
½ teaspoon vanilla

Oatcakes:
1 ½ cups flour
1 ½ cups rolled oats
½ teaspoon salt
½ cup shortening (room temperature)
½ cup butter (room temperature)
½ cup white sugar
½ teaspoon baking soda dissolved in
2 tablespoons of hot water

METHOD

Chop dates, add water and sugar, and cook for 10 minutes until softened. Remove from heat, add vanilla, and set aside to cool.

Mix flour, rolled oats, and salt, and set aside.

Cream shortening and butter together and add sugar. When blended, add flour/oat mixture and stir. Add the soda to the hot water and sprinkle over the mixture and blend until it all sticks together. Wrap in plastic wrap and chill for 15 minutes. Roll mixture thinly to about ⅛ inch thick. Cut with a 3-inch round cooker cutter.

Place a teaspoon of date mixture in the centre and fold the two half edges together to make a crescent. Repeat until all the dough is used.

Bake at 375°F for 15 minutes. Makes about 28 cookies.

Donna MacIver of Port Hawkesbury, Nova Scotia, is a woman who makes things happen. A devoted mother, grandmother, and great-grandmother, she has spent her life figuring out solutions to even the toughest challenges.

For years, she was the heart of her community as the owner of the local flower shop, Don's Flowers, working alongside her daughter to bring beauty and comfort to others. Whether for joyful celebrations or times of sorrow, Donna ensured that every arrangement was perfect, often working late into the night to never let anyone down.

When I met Donna at her daughter's home in Troy, she welcomed me with warm hospitality — and freshly baked oatcakes filled with dates, a cherished family recipe passed down through generations. As we sipped our tea, her grandson, Michael, serenaded us with his incredible voice, making the moment even more special.

Donna's granddaughter, Charlee, nominated her for this cookbook, sharing that Donna has always been the heart of their family's kitchen. Her fudge, squares, and endless baked treats aren't just delicious — they're made with love, creating memories that span generations. "Every single time I bake, I feel like I'm carrying on her tradition," Charlee says, a testament to the lasting impact of Donna's passion.

More than just a talented baker, Donna has built a legacy of love and togetherness, proving that the best recipes aren't just about ingredients — they're about the hands and hearts that make them.

Donna's advice to her grandchildren: *"Always remember, believe in yourself, as much as I believe in you; I can't promise to be here for the rest of your life, but I can promise to love you for the rest of mine – Love Nan xo"*

MAC'S NEIGHBOURLY ORANGE CRANBERRY SCONES

Mac Morin is a piano player, and an incredible stepdancer and the son of my friend Mary, a beautiful soul gone too soon. Mac is one of the finest piano players ever and has toured the world extensively with some of the best musicians. He loves a good cup of tea and when his neighbour Patty Greencorn dropped off these scones back in the early days of COVID, Mac was hooked. She happily shared the recipe and Mac has since made it his own and they are to die for!

INGREDIENTS

2 cups all-purpose flour
½ cup rolled oats (quick oats)
5 tablespoons white sugar (reserve 1 tablespoon for top)
¾ teaspoon baking powder
¾ teaspoon baking soda
¼ teaspoon salt
¾ cup butter
½ cup dried cranberries (or frozen)
1 cup buttermilk
Zest of one or two oranges
Zest of one lemon

METHOD

Preheat oven to 375°F. Combine the flour, rolled oats, 4 tablespoons sugar, baking powder, soda, and salt together. Cut the butter into smaller pieces and incorporate the butter into the dry ingredients with a pastry blender until all combined and crumbly. Sprinkle in the zest and then fold in the cranberries. Add the buttermilk and stir lightly with a wooden spoon until the dough comes together to form a ball. (The dough will be sticky but resist the temptation to overwork it.)

On a lightly floured surface, pat the dough into a large circle until it is about 1 inch thick. Sprinkle with the reserved tablespoon of sugar over the top. Cut the dough into wedges. Transfer the wedges to a parchment-lined baking sheet and bake for 22 minutes or until the edges are lightly browned. Cool on a wire rack. Best served warm on the day they are made.

APPLE CINNAMON STREUSEL MUFFINS

I make these regularly – so good.

INGREDIENTS

2 Granny Smith apples
2 cups bran flakes

Bowl 1:
1 ½ cups flour
¾ cup white sugar
1 tablespoon baking powder
1 teaspoon salt
¾ cup softened butter

Bowl 2:
2 eggs (whisked)
1 cup milk
1 ½ teaspoons cinnamon

Topping:
2 tablespoons brown sugar
1 teaspoon cinnamon
¼ - ½ cup chopped pecans

METHOD

Prepare ahead and have the apples and bran flakes ready. (You can use Kellogg's Cereal or the equivalent in either rolled oats, oat bran flakes, or wheat germ. I find bran flake cereal is best.) Dice the apples quite small (¼-inch pieces).

Preheat oven to 350°F.

Stir the dry ingredients together and then add all the softened butter. Mix well with your hands until mixture is nice and crumbly. Remove ½ cup and set aside for the topping.

Whisk together the ingredients in bowl 2 and then add the diced apple and the bran flakes. Mix together until combined. Mixture will be wet so set it aside so the bran flakes can absorb the liquid (about 5 minutes or so) and prepare the topping. To the ½ cup mixture that you set aside, add topping ingredients. Mix together and set aside.

When your mixture (bowl 2) has nicely absorbed the cereal, spoon into prepared muffin tins – you can either use muffin liners or spray your muffin tins. I prefer spraying them. This mixture will make about 14-15 muffins, or if you like a larger muffin, fill one tin.

Put about a slight tablespoon of topping on each muffin.

Bake for 22–25 minutes. Let rest for a few minutes before removing from muffin tin. So yummy with a cup of tea from the Cape Breton Tea Company!

Featured Grandmother

Eleanor Weldon

"She shows love through food and weekly family meals."

Eleanor's advice to her grandchildren: *"Time and tide wait for no man … and very few women."*

High on Lutes Mountain, overlooking the northwest side of Moncton, New Brunswick, Eleanor Weldon's home is a reflection of generations of love, craftsmanship, and family tradition. The land she lives on has been in her family for years, and her warmth and kindness make it feel like the heart of it all.

A soft-hearted and gentle woman, Eleanor is famous for one thing in particular — her old-fashioned buckwheat pancakes. Cooked on two well-seasoned cast-iron griddles atop her stove, these lacy-edged beauties are served with local maple syrup, fresh fruit, and a side of crispy bacon or sausages—your pick. Watching her gracefully pour and flip each pancake, you can feel the quiet joy she brings to her kitchen.

Eleanor and her husband built their home in their retirement, filling it with their shared handiwork. One of the most treasured pieces is the floor-to-ceiling cabinet he built to showcase her cherished dishes. But Eleanor's talent extends beyond the kitchen — she is a collector of vintage items spanning generations through family heirlooms and thrift store finds, giving them all a place of honour in her home.

Upstairs, two beautifully kept bedrooms — one for the girls, one for the boys — are dedicated to her grandchildren, complete with a dress-up trunk and everything needed for sleepovers. In her craft room, stacks of handmade pillowcases in every imaginable children's print await donation to the children's units at the two local hospitals.

Her granddaughter Laurel nominated her, sharing how Eleanor has always been the heart of their family, welcoming them all with open arms, baked goods, and hearty meals. "She showed me resilience through trying new recipes, always tweaking them to make them better. She taught me the fundamentals of baking and how food brings us together. She's just the best, and I love her so much."

Eleanor Weldon is a grandmother whose love is felt in every moment spent around her table.

OLD-FASHIONED BUCKWHEAT PANCAKES

Eleanor Weldon's recipe

INGREDIENTS

1 quart buttermilk
2 cups buckwheat flour*
1 cup all-purpose white flour
1 teaspoon salt
1 teaspoon baking soda

* A light and fine-textured buckwheat flour is recommended for this recipe.

METHOD

In a large pouring bowl or pitcher, whisk together buttermilk, buckwheat flour, and all-purpose flour. In a small amount of warm water, dissolve soda and salt, add to batter and whisk well. Mixture should be quite thin and pourable – if too thick, add warm water in small amounts.

Heat griddle until a bubble of water will bounce – cast-iron works best for these pancakes. Grease griddle with shortening.

Pour rounds of batter, cook until edges are firm and showing a bit dry, then turn and cook on other side. Edges should be lacy and uneven; if not, the griddle was not hot enough. These pancakes should be thin and delicate.

Serve hot with butter and maple syrup. Good with sausage, bacon, baked beans, and eggs. Fruit salad makes a nice finish for this meal.

Remembering Catherine Ann (MacDonald) MacDonnell

Catherine Ann (MacDonald) MacDonnell was from Mabou and was only 39 when cancer stole her from her husband and five children on December 26, 1994. I remember her well. She was a loving wife and mother and would have loved to have had the chance to be a grandmother today to her nine beautiful grandchildren. A yearly scholarship (MacDonnell Scholarship) has been set up at St. Francis Xavier University in Antigonish by her family. It is awarded to a community-minded female student with good marks, who embraces volunteerism.

Her daughter Jen (pictured here with her Mom) cherishes this recipe and I am so happy to share it here.

CATHERINE ANN'S APPLE MUFFINS

INGREDIENTS

Topping:
1 cup brown sugar
½ cup flour
2 teaspoons cinnamon
4 tablespoons melted butter

Small Bowl:
4 ½ cups flour
2 teaspoons baking soda
1 teaspoon salt

Large Bowl:
3 cups brown sugar
2 eggs
2 cups buttermilk
2 teaspoons vanilla
4 cups diced apples

METHOD

Mix the brown sugar, flour, and cinnamon and then add the melted butter and mix well. Set aside.

Mix together the flour, baking soda, and salt and set aside.

Whisk the eggs and add the brown sugar until well mixed. Add the buttermilk and vanilla and mix well. Add the dry ingredients and the apples and mix just until no flour can be seen.

Put liners in the muffin tins and fill to the top with batter and then sprinkle with topping. Bake at 350°F for approximately 25-28 minutes. Makes 2 dozen.

BANANA CHOCOLATE CHIP MUFFINS

A lovely singing guest on my show, Sheena Anderson-Geiger, shared this recipe. So yummy!

INGREDIENTS

Dry Ingredients:

1 1⁄3 cups rolled oats
2 cups all-purpose flour
1 cup white sugar
2 teaspoons baking powder
½ teaspoon baking soda
1 teaspoon salt
1 cup flax meal

Wet Ingredients:

2 eggs
1 cup milk
1⁄3 cup oil (corn oil or vegetable oil, or replace with apple sauce)
3 medium bananas (mashed) – about 1 cup
1 cup semi-sweet chocolate chips

METHOD

Set oven to 350°F.

Mix all dry ingredients and set aside.

Whisk the wet ingredients together and slowly add the dry ingredients. Drop into greased muffin tins filling each space about ¾ full. (Use muffin liners if preferred.) Bake for about 18 minutes. Makes about 2 dozen.

SOUPS, CHOWDERS, AND QUICK MEALS

Featured Grandmother

Leona MacInnis

""Nana's kitchen has always been a place of comfort and connection."

Leona's advice to her grandchildren:
"Make sure you clean up after yourself!"

LEONA'S SEAFOOD CHOWDER

Leona MacInnis' recipe

INGREDIENTS

¼ cup butter
2 onions (diced)
1 cup chopped celery
2 cups water
1 teaspoon chicken soup base
3 carrots (diced small)
3 large potatoes (diced small)
1 pound haddock
1 pound scallops
1 pound cooked lobster (about two shelled)
½ pound salmon

Roux:

2 tablespoons butter
2 tablespoons flour
2 cups whipping cream (18% fat)

METHOD

Melt the butter in a Dutch oven and add the onions and celery and sauté (about 10 minutes) over medium heat. Add the chicken soup base to the water and add to the onion mixture. Add in the diced potatoes and carrots.

When carrots and potatoes are just about cooked, add the uncooked fish (haddock, scallops, and salmon). Add the lobster once the other fish has cooked.

In a separate pot, make a roux of flour and butter over medium heat and cook for about 3-4 minutes whisking constantly. Slowly, introduce the cream and keep whisking until thickened (about 2 minutes). Add to the Dutch oven and stir slowly and the chowder will thicken. Add salt and pepper to your taste.

Leona MacInnis has spent a lifetime nourishing others, both in the kitchens of local restaurants and in the heart of her own home. A beloved cook in Cape Breton, she spent many years working at the Red Shoe Pub in Mabou, where her seafood chowder became nothing short of legendary. It wasn't just Red Shoe patrons who raved about her cooking — her family, friends, and neighbours also cherished the meals she lovingly prepared.

Her late husband, Richard MacInnis, a fisherman, was one of her biggest fans, along with their children and grandchildren. To her family, she is more than just a great cook — she is "Nana," a title that means the world to her eight grandchildren. As her granddaughter beautifully put it, *"Nana has always gone above and beyond to make our stays truly amazing. There has not been a single visit where she didn't express her love through her cooking and baking."* From pancakes at breakfast to homemade sugar cookies, brownies, biscuits, and rolls, her kitchen has always been a place of comfort and connection.

Since Richard's passing in August 2022, Leona's food has remained a steady presence, helping to keep the family close. Though the house may be quieter, and his seat on the couch may be empty, Nana's kitchen continues to bring warmth, love, and the feeling of home. Or, as another granddaughter simply put it, *"My nana has the warmest heart and the fullest freezer."* When Leona gave me the recipe, there were no amounts – that's how she cooks – from taste and looks – she knows how it should turn out. Now that's cooking!

POTATO, BACON, & CHEDDAR SOUP

I've made this my own and it's one of those recipes where you'd probably have all the ingredients already.

INGREDIENTS

5 slices bacon (cooked and diced)
3 tablespoons butter
1 medium onion, chopped fine
2 cloves minced garlic
5 medium/large potatoes (peeled and diced)
1 small carrot (diced small)
1 box (900 ml) chicken broth
Salt and pepper
2 cups milk (I use 2%)
½ cup blend cream (10% fat)
½ cup shredded cheddar
½ cup kernel corn (or more)

METHOD

Sauté the onion and garlic in the butter (about 5 minutes on medium-low heat) in a 5-quart Dutch oven. Add the potatoes and carrots to the onion mixture plus the chicken broth. Add salt and pepper to taste and bring to a boil. Simmer for about 20 minutes or until veggies are soft. When cooked, turn heat off and blend the soup with an immersion blender. Add the milk and cream and turn heat back on and bring to a simmer. Add most of the crumbled bacon and the shredded cheddar, corn. Mix until the cheddar is melted.

Serve it up and garnish as desired with a small dollop of sour cream, some crumbled bacon, parsley, and some chopped green onion.

ITALIAN WINTER SOUP

This recipe is a result of a mix of two recipes. I absolutely recommend this blend.

INGREDIENTS

2 tablespoons olive oil
1 pound lean ground beef
1 large onion, diced
4 garlic cloves, minced
1 box (900 ml) chicken broth
1 can herbed diced tomatoes (14.5 ounces)
1 can tomato sauce (14.5 ounces)
1 cup water
1 teaspoon dried basil
1 teaspoon Italian seasoning
Salt and pepper to taste
1 cup bowtie pasta * (see other pasta options below)
1 cup mozzarella cheese, grated
½ cup parmesan cheese, grated
½ cup cottage cheese or ricotta cheese
Fresh parsley

METHOD

In a Dutch oven on medium heat, place the oil and gently heat it, then add the beef and continue cooking until the beef is browned and crumbly. Slant the pot slightly to spoon out any excess fat. Add the diced onion and stir until it has softened. Add the minced garlic and sauté for 2-3 minutes. Add the chicken broth, diced tomatoes, tomato sauce, water, spices, and the salt and pepper. Bring to a boil and then turn heat down and simmer for about 5 minutes.

Add the bowtie pasta and continue simmering for another 15 minutes. Add some boiling water if soup needs to be thinned, according to your liking. I find it actually thickens a bit so more water or more broth may not be necessary.

Meanwhile, in a bowl, mix together the mozzarella, parmesan, and ricotta cheese and set aside until soup is ready to be served. (If using cottage cheese, put the ½ cup of cheese in a sieve above a bowl and use a fork to squeeze out the excess liquid).

Ladle soup into bowls and dollop with a scoop of the cheese mixture and top with some chopped parsley or some fresh basil. Serve with a nice, fresh roll slathered with butter, or better still, a slice of warmed herb bread.

**Pasta options:* If you don't have bowtie pasta, cook some of your favourite pasta (rotini, fusilli, macaroni, etc.) according to package directions and then add the drained cooked pasta to your soup at the end of the 20 minutes of simmering. Bowtie pasta is so thin that it cooks in the 15-minute simmer time, but other pasta needs to be cooked on its own before adding to the soup.

CORN CHOWDER

An easy chowder and always a favourite. Thank you to friend Gerarda Bonvie for sharing.

INGREDIENTS

3 cups potatoes, diced
1 cup celery, chopped
1 cup carrots, grated
1 cup onion
2 cups water
4 slices bacon, diced
¼ cup flour
2 ¼ cups milk
13 ½-ounce can evaporated milk
14-ounce can creamed corn
1 can kernel corn
1 teaspoon salt
½ teaspoon pepper
⅛-¼ teaspoon cayenne pepper

METHOD

Cover and cook vegetables in a large saucepan. Do not drain.

Fry bacon in frying pan.

Mix flour in with bacon; stir in both milks until mixture boils, then add to potato mixture. Add corn, salt, and peppers. Stir and heat through.

Makes 10 cups.

Featured Grandmother

Minna MacDonald

"Nothing makes her happier than baking for family and friends."

MINNA'S SWEET AND SOUR MEATBALLS

Minna MacDonald's recipe

INGREDIENTS

3 pounds ground beef
1 pound ground pork
1 grated onion
½ cup chopped parsley
½ cup chopped celery
3 teaspoons salt
½ teaspoon pepper
6 bread slices soaked in
  1 ½ cups milk (warmed)

Sauce:
2 cups brown sugar
1 cup vinegar
1 cup water
1 ½ tablespoons dry mustard
1 ½ cup ketchup
1 cups crushed pineapple
½ cup pineapple juice
3 tablespoons cornstarch

METHOD

Mix all together and form into balls. Makes about 5-6 dozen. Brown in frying pan and drain fat.

Mix sauce ingredients together and pour over meatballs. Bake at 350°F for 1–1½ hours.

Minna MacDonald, from Antigonish, Nova Scotia, has been making headlines in her kitchen for years, delighting family and friends with her incredible cooking. Whether she's whipping up a delicious homemade dish, tending to her vibrant flowerpots, swimming in her backyard pool, or soaking up the sun during winters down south, Minna knows how to embrace life to the fullest. She is all about creating meaningful experiences, and food has always been at the heart of those moments.

Before retiring, Minna spent many years as a dedicated nurse, offering care and compassion to those she cared for in the hospital. Her kindness and gentle ways left a lasting impact on her patients and colleagues alike. That same nurturing spirit carries into her kitchen, where she continues to care for others through her love of cooking.

During the first year of COVID, Minna and her granddaughter Emerson made a special tradition of tuning in to *Tunes and Wooden Spoons* every Sunday. It became their shared ritual, a way to connect through music and food during uncertain times. Minna even reached out to share how much they enjoyed the show, passing along a few of her treasured recipes — ones that I still make to this day. She and her husband, Jimmy, have built a life filled with joy, love, and plenty of good meals.

Her granddaughter Emerson nominated Minna, saying, *"Nothing makes her happier than cooking for her family and friends. She loves preparing meals and takes great joy in sharing her recipes with her grandchildren. She instilled a love of cooking and baking in me. The kitchen is definitely one of her happy places."*

Minna MacDonald's legacy is one of warmth, tradition, and the simple joy of gathering around the table, where love is served with every meal.

Minna's advice to her grandchildren:
"Put your best foot forward and always do your best. Be respectful, honest, and kind to others."

G'S SQUASH, CARROT, AND APPLE SOUP

Another delightful soup from Gerarda Bonvie.

INGREDIENTS

1 butternut squash, oven-roasted, peeled and chopped *
2 tablespoons olive oil
4 onions, chopped
4 cloves garlic, minced
3 large carrots, peeled and chopped
3 large apples, peeled and chopped
1 cup apple juice
4 cups chicken stock
½ teaspoon nutmeg
2 teaspoons curry
Salt, pepper, and parsley to taste
½ cup cream (optional)

METHOD

In a large saucepan, sauté onions and garlic in oil. Add all ingredients (except the cream) and bring to a boil, cooking until vegetables are tender. Blend (hand blender works well). Add cream and stir just before serving.

* To roast the squash, pre-heat oven to 250°F. Cut squash in half and remove seeds. Place inside down on parchment-lined cookie sheet. Bake for about 40 minutes or until tender. Peel and chop.

Featured Grandmother

Sharon MacGillivray

"We love her and want everyone else to know too."

SHARON'S SIGNATURE SEAFOOD CHOWDER

Sharon MacGillivray's recipe

INGREDIENTS

3 pounds haddock (cubed)
3 pounds scallops (cut large scallops in ½)
3 (340 gram) bags raw shrimp
2 cups cooked lobster (cubed)
2 cans baby clams (drained)
2 cans crabmeat (drained)
6 cups potatoes (cubed)
1 ½ cups onion (diced)
1 ½ cups celery (diced)
1 ½ cups carrot (diced)
2 tablespoons minced fresh garlic
1 ½ teaspoons parsley
2 tablespoons + 2 teaspoons seafood seasoning
1 ½ teaspoons summer savory
2 bay leaves
Salt and pepper
3 tablespoons butter
4 cups white wine
4 cups blend cream (or equivalent 10% fat)

METHOD

In a large pot, melt butter, sauté onions, celery, garlic and spices for a few minutes on low heat.

Add white wine, haddock, scallops and shrimp and simmer on low heat until fish is cooked. Add lobster, baby clams ,and crabmeat.

In a separate pot, cook potatoes and carrots in a small amount of water until tender, but don't overcook. Drain potato and carrots.

Combine fish and potatoes. Add cream to a heavy pot and heat on low to medium until heated. Add hot cream and simmer the chowder for 10 minutes. Do not boil. Remove bay leaves.

Nestled in the beautiful countryside of Lanark, Nova Scotia, Sharon MacGillivray's home is a place of warmth, welcome, and the most incredible home cooking. It was no surprise that I received multiple nominations from her grandchildren — each one a heartfelt testament to how deeply she is loved and admired.

"Gramma always has open doors and feeds everyone. Her food is the best I've ever tasted," wrote one. Another shared, *"She is the matriarch of the family. She keeps us all together. When I think of the word home, she is the person who comes to mind."*

Sharon grew up as the seventh child in a family of 14 children, (3 girls and 11 boys! – poor Sharon!) but yet she didn't mind taking on the role of caretaker from a young age. To this day, her siblings travel from across the world to visit her, and even their children call her Gramma. She is the heart of the family, always putting others first. Her kitchen is the centre of it all, a place where delicious meals are constantly in the works, and where visitors are greeted with a warm hug and a full plate. Her legendary seafood chowder, praised as "the best on the planet," is made with care and precision, a true masterpiece of East Coast flavours.

During my visit, I had the privilege of watching Sharon in her element, standing beside her at the stove as she prepared her signature dish with the ease of a master. Surrounded by family, laughter, and love, we eventually sat down for tea and a homemade treat — one more cherished moment in a home filled with them.

As one of her grandchildren put it, *"My Gramma is the most special person in the world."* And after spending time in her home, it's clear why she holds such a treasured place in so many hearts.

Sharon's advice to her grandchildren: *"You're loved and valued, no matter what."*

CHEATER TOMATO SOUP

If you like homemade tomato soup, but don't want to roast your veggies, try this version – you won't be disappointed.

INGREDIENTS

1 20-ounce can crushed tomatoes
1 15-ounce can tomato sauce
1 237-ml container whipping cream (35% fat)
1 473-ml container blend (cereal) cream (10% fat)
½ cup butter
1 can cream of chicken soup
1 tablespoon basil
Garlic salt
Garlic powder
Salt and pepper

METHOD

In a 5–6-quart Dutch oven, put the crushed tomatoes, tomato sauce, chicken soup, and butter. Stir frequently until the butter has melted. Add the whipping cream and blend cream and stir well. Add the basil, garlic salt, garlic powder, salt, pepper, boil, and simmer on low for 15 minutes.

Featured Grandmother

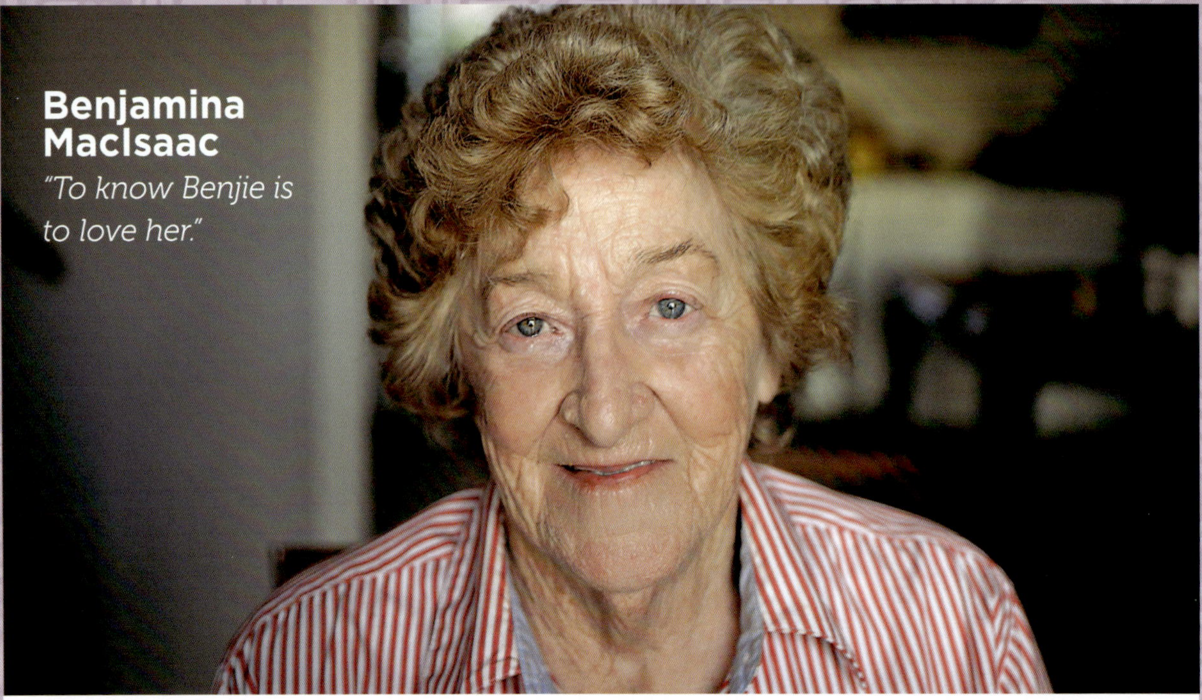

Benjamina MacIsaac

"To know Benjie is to love her."

Benjamina MacIsaac of Inverness, Nova Scotia, is a mother, grandmother, great-grandmother, and a true force of nature. At 87, there is absolutely nothing old about her — she is as lively and full of energy as ever.

I still remember her as my elementary school teacher (and that wasn't yesterday!), and she has left a lasting impact on countless young minds over the years. During our visit, she shared a few stories from her early teaching days, including the joys (and tribulations) of dealing with "spilt milk"— stories that had us both laughing.

When I first arrived at her home, she "didn't get the memo." My plan was to make her famous seafood supreme casserole from scratch or at least have one ready for photos — but that wasn't the case. When she realized it, the giggles began, and they didn't stop. We were all in stitches, and I left with a promise that we'd try again. A couple of weeks later, Benjamina and her dear husband, Junior, showed up at my home, ingredients in tow, ready to set things right. This time, we still had a few laughs, but we got the casserole made and into the oven — and it was absolutely incredible.

"If at first you don't succeed, try, try again," as the saying goes. But with Benjamina, it's never about success or failure — it's about joy, love, and sharing moments with those around her. She is a treasure, a beloved member of her community, and a shining example of how to embrace life with humour, kindness, and an open heart. Keep doing what you're doing, Benji — you inspire us all.

SEAFOOD SUPREME CASSEROLE

Benjamina MacIsaac's recipe

INGREDIENTS

2 cans (4½-ounce each) shrimp, drained
1 can lobster meat, drained
1 can (6-ounce) crab meat, drained (or substitute with scallops, thawed if frozen)
⅓ cup butter
2 cups sliced fresh mushrooms
¼ cup chopped onions
⅓ cup flour
½ teaspoon salt
1 ¾ cups milk
½ pint cream
1 cup crushed rice crisp cereal
2 tablespoons melted butter

Note: I often use frozen seafood (thawed) — feel free to customize to your preference!

METHOD

Preheat oven to 375°F.

Place seafood in a bowl and set aside.

In a large saucepan, melt butter over medium heat. Add mushrooms and onions, sautéing gently until softened. Blend in flour and salt, stirring well.

Remove from heat and gradually stir in milk and cream. Return to heat and cook, stirring constantly, until thickened. Gently fold in seafood, then transfer mixture to a 2-quart casserole dish.

In a small bowl, combine crushed rice crisp cereal with melted butter. Sprinkle the cereal mixture over the casserole.

Bake for 30 minutes or until bubbly and golden brown on top.

Benjamina's advice to her grandchildren:
"Experience is yesterday's answer to today's problems."

MULLIGATAWNY SOUP

This recipe is from Gerarda Bonvie (our son Mitchell's neighbour). This soup has Indian roots and is spicy and delicious.

INGREDIENTS

4 tablespoons butter
2 cups celery, chopped
½ cup onion, diced
2 tablespoons flour
2 tablespoons curry powder
4 cups chicken broth
1 bay leaf
¼ cup apple, peeled and diced
½ tsp lemon zest
¼ teaspoon salt (add more if using homemade chicken broth)
¼ teaspoon pepper
¼ teaspoon thyme
½ cup cooked white rice
2 cups chicken, cooked and chopped
½ cup coconut milk

METHOD

Sauté veggies until tender, but not brown. Stir in flour and curry powder, cook for 1 minute. Add all ingredients down to (and including) thyme; simmer for 15 minutes. Add rice and chicken, heat through. Add coconut milk just before serving.

FRENCH ONION SOUP

I got this recipe from a dear online friend who followed Tunes and Wooden Spoons *from the very beginning. Ann McColm was from B.C., was an amazing visual artist, and loved to cook and share recipes with friends. May she rest in peace.*

INGREDIENTS

4 tablespoons butter
4 pounds onions (sliced thin)
1 ¾ teaspoons salt (divided)
1 teaspoon sugar
1 cup dry red wine
8 cups beef broth
4 sprigs fresh thyme
2 bay leaves
¾ teaspoon pepper, divided
One baguette – enough to cover the soup top and cut into 1-inch cubes
3 tablespoons extra virgin olive oil
8 ounces Gruyere cheese, shredded (about 2 cups)
½ cup shredded parmesan cheese

METHOD

Melt the butter in a Dutch oven over medium-high heat. Stir in the onions, 1 teaspoon salt, and sugar. Cover and cook, stirring occasionally, until onions release their liquid and are all translucent – this should take about 20 minutes.

Uncover and cook until liquid has evaporated and browned bits start to form on bottom of pot – 5 to 10 minutes. Reduce heat to medium and continue to cook, uncovered, until onions are caramel coloured (about 35-40 minutes) – and keep stirring with a wooden spoon as the brown bits form on the bottom of the pot and spreading the onions into even layers after stirring. If the onion starts scorching, reduce the heat on your stove to medium-low.

Stir in the wine, scraping all the browned bits, and cook until nearly evaporated (takes about 1 minute). Stir in the broth, thyme sprigs, bay leaves, ½ teaspoon pepper, and ½ teaspoon salt. Increase heat to high and bring to a boil. Reduce heat to medium-low and simmer, uncovered, for 30 minutes. While onions simmer, preheat oven to 350°F. Toss the baguette cubes, oil, the remaining ¼ teaspoon salt, the remaining ¼ teaspoon pepper together in a bowl, and place the cubes on a parchment-lined cookie sheet. Bake until golden and crisp – about 15-18 minutes. Remove sheet from oven and set aside.

Increase the oven temperature to 500°F.

Set out six 12-ounce oven-safe crocks on a parchment-lined cookie sheet. Discard the thyme sprigs and bay leaves and season the soup with salt and pepper to taste. Divide the soup evenly among the crocks (about 1 ½ cups each). Divide the 1 cup Gruyere evenly among the crocks, and top with the croutons, and sprinkle with Parmesan cheese. Bake until cheeses are melted and soup is bubbly around edges (about 5-7 minutes). Let cool for 5 minutes before serving.

ACADIAN FRICOT FROM POINT CROSS

LE FRICOT ACADIEN DE LA "FARME"

This Acadian staple dish has been in my friend Betty Ann Cormier's family for generations. No one can be sure if it is truly an Acadian dish or if it has influences from the Indigenous peoples who helped early settlers survive the first frigid, tough winters. With very little access to ingredients, Acadians used the basic staples available to them at the time. Nowadays, fricots have evolved within communities and families. This dish can be jazzed up with veggies or dumplings to meet individual tastes.

INGREDIENTS

2 boneless chicken breasts or legs/thighs (cubed and cooked – see below*) or 3 cups of leftover diced chicken
6 large russet potatoes, peeled and diced into bite-size pieces
6 cups water
1 tablespoon butter
1 large onion, diced
2 cubes of chicken bouillon
1 teaspoon salt
½ teaspoon pepper
1 teaspoon chicken seasoning**
2 tablespoons salted chives***

METHOD

In a large pot over medium heat, melt the butter and add the diced onion and sauté until onion is caramelized. Add the bouillon cubes and 1 cup water and stir until cubes are dissolved. Add the 6 cups of water and the diced potatoes. Add the cooked chicken. Let the ingredients come to a boil, lower the heat to medium, and continue cooking until potatoes are cooked through. Rinse the chives and dice and sprinkle with salt. Add the salted chives, chicken spice, salt and pepper. Simmer for another 15-20 minutes on medium heat.

Once ready to serve, place in a soup bowl and add green onions for garnish (and taste)! Goes well with homemade biscuits or fresh homemade bread. Yields a meal for 4 people. Enjoy!

*If you haven't cooked the chicken, cut the chicken into bite-size pieces and put in a pot with 2 cups water and a pinch of salt. Bring to a boil and continue to boil for 10 minutes and set aside.

** If chicken seasoning is not available, use summer savoury as a replacement.

*** Salted chives are not available in stores (that I know of) but are prepared in Acadian homes by salting the chives in layers in a jar, covering in water, and storing it for up to a year.

Featured Grandmother

Debbie Kennedy

"She taught us to bake the best chocolate chip cookies!"

Debbie's advice to her grandchildren:

"Baking with grandchildren is not about recipes, it's about creativity, life skills, and making memories to last a lifetime."

CHICKEN AND BROCCOLI CASSEROLE

Debbie Kennedy's recipe

INGREDIENTS

4-6 boneless chicken breasts
1-2 heads broccoli
1 can cream of chicken soup
½ cup water
½ cup mayonnaise
½ tablespoon lemon juice
½ teaspoon curry
½ cup grated cheddar cheese

METHOD

Cook chicken breasts and cut into bite-sized pieces. Steam broccoli until tender and drain. Place broccoli in bottom of casserole dish. Layer chicken on top.

Mix remaining ingredients and pour over chicken and broccoli. Sprinkle with breadcrumbs or crushed corn flakes.

Bake at 350°F for 45 minutes. If you like a little more sauce, add another can of soup and ½ cup water.

If you've ever heard the song "Out on the Mira," then you can picture the breathtaking place Debbie Kennedy calls home. At the Mira, nestled in that picturesque setting, Debbie welcomed me with open arms — and the most incredible kitchen aromas. With a bubbling rice casserole and a comforting chicken broccoli bake in the oven, it was a win-win situation from the moment I walked in.

What made the visit even sweeter were her three darling grandchildren — Blake, Sadie, and Lainey, ages 9, 7, and 1. It's clear that these little ones adore their Nana, and their shared love of baking is something truly special. Even Lainey, the youngest, knows when Nana is about to bake, ready with her spoon in hand to stir the pot. Their heartfelt nomination said it best: *"We've been baking with our Nana ever since we were old enough to hold a spoon. She taught us to make the best chocolate chip cookies, banana loaf, shortbread cookies, bread pretzels, and cinnamon rolls. She is the most caring Nana we could ever ask for and is always up for baking with us every week."*

A nurse by profession, Debbie has spent her life caring for others, a role that extends far beyond her career. She and her husband love to go RVing, spending their summers at Inverness Beach, where sunshine and sandy shores become their home away from home. She shared with me a special photo of her beloved dog, recently passed, taken on that very beach — a loss still deeply felt.

Young at heart and full of love, Debbie's world revolves around her family, especially those grandchildren who light up her life. And as I saw firsthand, the warmth of her heart is matched only by the warmth of her kitchen.

MEDITERRANEAN RAGOUT

One of the recipes that Minna MacDonald shared with me.

INGREDIENTS

- 2 tablespoons olive oil
- 6 Italian sausages sliced into 1-inch pieces (I used Italian sausage with basil or try hot Italian sausage)
- 4 boneless chicken breasts (cut into 1-inch cubes)
- 1 medium onion (chopped into 1-inch pieces)
- 1 green pepper (seeded and sliced into 1-inch pieces)
- 1 red pepper (seeded and sliced into 1-inch pieces)
- 1 (8-ounce) package of mushrooms (cut the mushrooms in half)
- 6 garlic cloves (coarsely chopped)
- 3 large potatoes peeled or scrubbed and cut into 1-inch pieces.
- 1 can diced tomatoes
- 1 box chicken broth (900 ml)
- 1 teaspoon oregano
- 2 tablespoons dried basil (or ½ cup fresh basil)*

* If using fresh basil, don't add it at Step 3. Instead, wait until all is cooked (after the 30 minutes) and then add the fresh basil – cover and let rest for 5 minutes until the basil marries into the rest of the goodness.

METHOD

Food Preparation: I find it best to have your meat cubed and your vegetables all prepared BEFORE you begin making the ragout.

Step 1: In a Dutch oven, heat the oil and add the sliced sausages until browned on both sides (3-4 minutes). Remove to a plate, add the chicken cubes to the Dutch oven, brown slightly on all sides (3-4 minutes), remove from pan and add to the plate of sausages.

Step 2: Add the onion, peppers, mushrooms, and garlic to the Dutch oven and stir occasionally while the flavours collide (about 3 minutes).

Step 3: Add the remaining ingredients and stir, scraping any bits in the bottom off the pan and then add the sausage and chicken (and any juices that escaped onto the plate). Bring all to a boil and then reduce heat, cover the pot, and simmer the ragout for 30 minutes. Add salt and pepper to taste.

FETTUCCINE ALFREDO WITH CHICKEN

Clara Bonvie lives next door to our son and daughter-in-law Mitch and Laura. Clara makes this delicious Alfredo sauce often and loves serving it to her sister Abby, and her parents, Herb and Gerarda.

INGREDIENTS

Chicken:

4 tablespoons butter
2 chicken breasts
1 teaspoon garlic powder
1 teaspoon onion powder
1 teaspoon paprika
1 teaspoon Italian seasoning
½ teaspoon cayenne
Salt and pepper to taste

Sauce:

½ cup butter
5 cloves garlic, minced
2 cups heavy cream
1 teaspoon Italian seasoning
¼ teaspoon nutmeg
Salt and pepper to taste
2 cups parmesan, grated
½ cup Romano cheese, grated
¼ cup chopped fresh parsley
Fettuccine, 1 box cooked as per instructions (save ½ pasta water)

METHOD

Melt butter in a frying pan. Add the garlic powder, onion powder, paprika, Italian seasoning, cayenne, and salt and pepper. Cook chicken in the butter and seasonings until internal temperature reaches 165°F. Remove, slice, and set aside.

To make sauce, melt butter in frying pan. Add garlic and cook for 1-2 minutes. Add cream and bring to a boil, stirring constantly. Add Italian seasoning, nutmeg, salt, pepper, and stir. Add both cheeses and stir until melted. Stir in parsley and pasta water. Stir in cooked fettuccine, plate, and top with sliced chicken and garnish with parsley.

Featured Grandfather

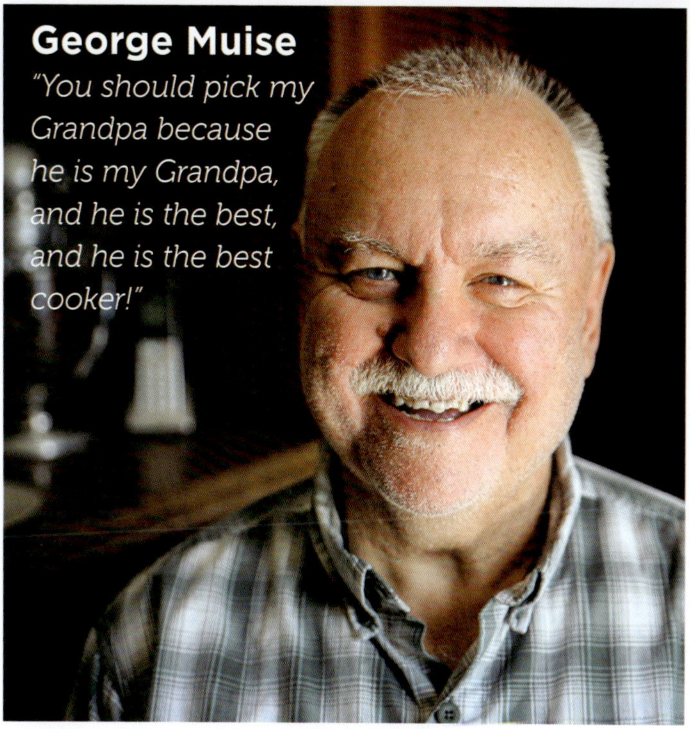

George Muise of Glace Bay, Nova Scotia, likely never expected to hear back from me. But when I was scrolling through the hundreds of comments on one of my *Facebook* livestreams — where I had announced plans to feature Maritime grandmothers in my next cookbook — his comment jumped out at me: "What about Grandpas?" That was the lightbulb moment. Why not!

So, I sent George a private message and asked if he would be one of two grandfathers featured. I think I caught him off guard, but eventually, he agreed. And let me tell you — I am so glad he did. This man should be a chef. His lasagna is nothing short of extraordinary, as are his lemon squares.

Watching him cook was like watching an artist at work. With great care and precision, he prepared every element: cooking the lasagna noodles to perfection (no oven-ready shortcuts for him!), lightly spraying them with oil and layering them between sheets of parchment to prevent sticking. His sauce was simmered for hours the day before (unlike my usual 15-minute version), filling his home with the most incredible aroma.

When it came time to assemble, he meticulously fit each noodle into the pan, even cutting them with scissors for a precise fit. And of course, he finished it off with freshly zested real Parmesan — none of the store-bought pre-grated stuff. His wife, Karen, is a very lucky lady, and she accepts and loves that her husband loves to cook – not just for her but for their children and grandchildren, the loves of their lives.

As if that lasagna he was working on wasn't impressive enough, he had a second lasagna already baked and waiting for us to taste. Every bite was a masterpiece. My admiration for George only grew as I saw the love and joy he puts into cooking for his family and friends. He originally called his recipe simply Lasagna, but I had to rename it — because it was magnificent. Lasagna Grandiosa was born.

Hail to you, George—what an incredible experience!

LASAGNA GRANDIOSA

George Muise's recipe

INGREDIENTS

- 1 pound Italian sausage (casings removed)
- 1 pound lean or medium ground beef
- 1 cup finely diced onion
- 3 cloves crushed garlic
- 2 teaspoons fresh basil (or 1 ½ teaspoons dried)
- 1 teaspoon fennel seeds
- 1 teaspoon Italian seasoning
- 1 teaspoon salt
- ½ teaspoon black pepper
- 1 teaspoon red pepper flakes (optional)
- ¼ cup chopped fresh Italian or curly parsley
- 1 tablespoon balsamic vinegar
- 2 tablespoons white sugar
- 1 28-ounce can diced tomatoes
- 2 6-ounce cans tomato paste
- 2 bottles (approx. 300 ml each) of Italian sausage pasta sauce (or favourite pasta sauce)
- 16 ounce ricotta cheese
- 1 egg
- ½ teaspoon salt

METHOD

In a large pot or Dutch oven, cook the sausage until brown. Use a potato masher to ensure the pieces are broken up small. Remove the cooked sausage and set aside. Cook the ground beef over medium heat until browned. Remove the cooked beef and set aside. Cook the onions (in the same pot) until translucent, add the garlic, basil, fennel seeds, Italian seasoning, salt, pepper, 2 tablespoons of parsley, balsamic vinegar, and sugar. Add the sausage and ground beef back to the pot.

Next, stir in canned tomatoes, tomato paste, and pasta sauce. Add a little water if sauce is too thick. Simmer for at least 2 hours. After 1 hour, taste the sauce and adjust seasoning if required.

Mix the ricotta cheese, egg, remaining parsley, and salt. Set aside.

Preheat oven to 350°F.

Cook the lasagna noodles as directed minus 2 minutes. Drain, rinse with cold water, and sprinkle with extra virgin olive oil. Separate and lay chilled noodles on a large plate (OR use oven-ready noodles if desired).

Layering: The number of layers will depend on the pan depth. Three layers will work for a usual 9x13-inch pan. If pan is deeper, add layers accordingly. If using a larger pan, more noodles need to be cooked.

Spread enough sauce on the bottom of baking dish to completely cover the bottom. This will ensure the lasagna will not stick. Arrange 4 noodles in the pan and cover as much of the bottom of the pan as possible without overlapping noodles. Trim noodles with kitchen shears if necessary to get a good fit. Spread half of the ricotta cheese mixture on top of noodles. Spread some grated mozzarella cheese on top and add about ¼ cup grated parmesan cheese. Top with a layer of sauce.

Place 4 noodles on top of previous layer. Spread the remaining ricotta cheese mixture and add shredded mozzarella and parmesan as before. Top with sauce. Place the remaining noodles on top of the previous layer. Cover the noodles with sauce. Spread enough shredded mozzarella to completely cover the sauce. Sprinkle about ¼ cup grated parmesan cheese on top. Cover with aluminum foil (it helps to spray the foil with cooking spray before covering so it does not stick.)

Bake at 350°F for 30 minutes. Remove foil and bake for another 30 minutes until golden brown. Let the lasagna rest for 15-20 minutes before cutting and serving. The lasagna can be made ahead and refrigerated for up to 2 days before baking or you can make ahead and freeze for up to 3 months.

George's advice to his grandchildren:
"Give 100 percent effort in everything you do, always love the unique person you are, and above all – be kind."

MJ'S MEATLOAF

Just a simple meatloaf with a taste of sweet and sour. Our family loves it.

INGREDIENTS

2 pounds lean ground beef
1 cup breadcrumbs
½ medium onion, grated
1 egg
Salt and pepper

Sauce:
About 1 cup ketchup
½ cup brown sugar
¼ cup white vinegar

METHOD

Mix ground beef, breadcrumbs, onion, egg, and salt and pepper together with your hands until combined, and set aside.

Mix sauce ingredients well. Add half to the meat mixture and mix together.

Press lightly into a loaf pan (about 9x5-inch). If using a non-stick pan, it doesn't need to be buttered, but if not, butter the pan or use cooking spray.

Pour the other half of the sauce over the top and spread lightly. Cover with foil wrap. Bake at 350°F for about an hour.

OLLIE'S SMASH BURGER PATTY MELTS

My grandson Oliver Stanley loves to cook and make delicious snacks and meals for himself, his brothers, and his friends. He has cooked in the kitchens of popular restaurants, and he enrolled in culinary school for 2025. I thought it would be great for him to share one of his favourite suppers in G-Ma's cookbook!

INGREDIENTS

1-2 pounds lean ground beef
2 medium onions (sliced)
Salt and pepper
Garlic powder
American cheese
2 slices of rye bread OR
  Texas toast bread
Butter

METHOD

Shape the ground beef into several patties and using the smooth side of a meat tenderizer or the bottom of a glass, make the patties very thin – ¼ inch or less.

Best if using a cast iron frying pan, place sliced onions into the hot and buttered frying pan and sauté until caramelized. Place the onions off to the side and place the patties into the hot pan. Season on all sides with salt, pepper, and garlic powder and fry until cooked through and nice and brown on all sides. Remove the onions and patties from the pan.

Butter the bread as you would for grilled cheese sandwiches, and place the cooked patties, onions, and cheese between the buttered slices of bread and grill until nice and brown.

Featured Grandmother

Anne Boudreau

"Nana keeps all nine of her grandkids fully stocked with cookies and muffins all year round. When we visit her house, we know there will always be a sweet treat for us. Her warm cookies warm our hearts."

CRESCENT ITALIAN BATA

Anne Boudreau's recipe

INGREDIENTS

1 pound lean ground beef
1 cup fresh mushrooms, chopped
½ cup chopped onion
¼ teaspoon salt
½ teaspoon pepper
1 cup tomato sauce
1 cup shredded cheddar cheese
8-ounce can of crescent rolls
½ cup sour cream
¼ teaspoon oregano
¼ teaspoon sweet basil

METHOD

Brown the ground beef along with the mushrooms and onions. Add the salt and pepper and stir, and add the tomato sauce. Place in a casserole dish and top with cheese.

Mix the sour cream with the oregano and basil and place about 1 tablespoon of the sour cream mixture in each of the crescent roll and then roll up and place on top of the casserole.

Bake at 375°F for 30 minutes.

Anne's advice to her grandchildren: *Excellence is not found in being the best, but in doing your best.*

I had the absolute pleasure of visiting Anne Boudreau in her charming home in New Waterford, Nova Scotia. From the moment I walked through the door, her warmth and kindness were undeniable — Anne is one of those rare souls whose beauty shines just as brightly from within as it does on the outside.

To give us full reign of the kitchen, she lovingly relegated her husband, Cyril, to his man cave in the garage. But that didn't stop her from talking about him with such affection — especially about their shared love of dancing. If there's music and a dance floor, you can bet Anne and Cyril will be there, twirling together with joy.

Her love for her family was evident in every word she spoke and in every carefully prepared meal she serves. She is incredibly blessed to have all nine of her grandchildren living nearby, which makes Nana a very happy lady.

Her home, pristine and beautifully kept, felt like a museum of love — every item had its place, and it radiated the same grace and care that Anne carries herself with. And, of course, Anne herself was stunning, dressed in her finest as if hosting a grand occasion.

For our visit, she shared a simple yet delicious recipe — a quick meal made with ground beef and crescent rolls. When I sat down to enjoy lunch with her, it was so good that I've made it twice since! Sometimes, the best dishes are the ones made with love and shared with family.

Spending time with Anne was a gift — the gentle way she spoke, the way she shared her stories, and the love that filled her home were all unforgettable. And Anne, I know where you live — so don't be surprised if I show up for another visit one day!

CHICKEN WINGS à la SAWYER

Sawyer Glencross – a teenager from Antigonish and a friend of our son and daughter-in-law (Mitch and Laura) – made this on Tunes and Wooden Spoons Facebook *livestream. He loves to cook, and this recipe has become the recipe of choice when making chicken wings.*

INGREDIENTS

2-3 dozen wings
2 tablespoons brown sugar
1 ½ teaspoons salt
1 ½ teaspoons paprika
1 ½ teaspoons garlic powder
1 teaspoon chili powder
½ teaspoon black pepper
½ teaspoon oregano

Sauce:
½ cup salted butter
2 cups ketchup
¼ cup brown sugar
¼ teaspoon paprika
½ cup apple cider vinegar
2 tablespoons honey
Little bit of Worcestershire sauce
Juice of half a lemon
Little bit of hot sauce
Tiny bit of liquid smoke

METHOD

BBQ should be pre-heated to 470°F OR a traditional oven should be pre-heated to 425°F.

Mix the sugar, salt, paprika, garlic powder, chilli powder, pepper, and oregano together. Fully coat each wing and let them sit for about 15 minutes.

BBQ: Place the wings on the BBQ and flip about every 10-12 minutes.

Oven: Place the wings on baking sheets lined with parchment paper. Flip the wings at around the 30-minute mark.

While the wings are cooking, prepare the sauce. Mix all the ingredients together and bring to a bubble over medium-high heat.

When the wings are almost done, coat with sauce and cook for another 10 minutes. The total cooking time from start to finish should be about an hour. Internal temperature should be at least 165°F.

Featured Grandmother

Louise MacLean

""My best memories with my nana have always been in the kitchen."

CHICKEN FRIED RICE

Louise MacLean's recipe

INGREDIENTS

- 2 medium or 1 large boneless chicken breast, cubed.
- 3 cups uncooked, long grain rice (not instant)
- 2 cans consommé soup
- 2 cans water
- 1/3 cup oil
- 1/2 cup green pepper, diced
- 1 can drained mushrooms
- 1/2 cup onion, diced
- 1/2 cup diced celery
- 6 tablespoons soy sauce
- 6 tablespoons molasses
- 6 heaping tablespoons brown sugar

METHOD

Place the cubed chicken in a frying pan on medium heat, turning frequently to lightly brown on all sides. When cooked through, set aside.

Stir rice, soup, water, and oil together. Add the vegetables and stir.

Combine soya sauce, molasses, and brown sugar. Add to the rice and vegetables mixture, along with the browned chicken. Stir to combine and cook in casserole dish at 350°F for 1 hour. Enjoy!

Louise's advice to her grandchildren: *"Always remember your roots! Never let money or power change you!"*

Louise MacLean welcomed us into her Glace Bay home with open arms, and from the moment we stepped inside, we felt like old friends. Not only is she a talented cook and baker, but Louise is also a gifted crafter, and I was touched to receive a beautifully embroidered dishtowel with "Mary Janet's Kitchen" stitched on it — something I will cherish forever.

Her home is warm and inviting, but it was her sunroom that truly captured my heart, with its wraparound windows, cozy chairs, and perfect spots for reading, knitting, crocheting, tole painting, quilting, or watching TV. I saw one of her quilts and it was absolutely stunning!

Of course, the kitchen was where the magic happened. Louise treated us to her delicious chicken fried rice, the recipe she contributed for this book, but she didn't stop there — she prepared a full meal, complete with homemade meatballs, rolls, and sweet treats. Her sister Sheila joined us, bringing along caramel cones, which you'll also find in these pages.

The love of food and family is clearly something Louise has passed down, as her granddaughter Samantha shared in her heartfelt nomination. Samantha's fondest memories are of baking alongside her Nana, who always made sure she felt included — even creating gluten-free and dairy-free treats just for her. "She has always given back to others through her superpower of baking," Samantha wrote.

Sitting with Louise and Sheila, it was easy to see why she is so treasured. The warmth of her kitchen and her heart made this visit unforgettable.

MJ'S BREAKFAST CASSEROLE

This recipe comes from my cousin Mary Jessie MacLellan in Antigonish – it is a staple in her house and now in mine.

INGREDIENTS

8 frozen hash brown patties
4 cups shredded cheddar
1 pound cubed cooked ham (about 4 cups)
7 eggs
1 cup milk
½ teaspoon salt
½ teaspoon pepper
½ teaspoon ground mustard

METHOD

Place patties in a single layer in a buttered 9x13-inch pan. Sprinkle with the cheese and ham.

Beat the eggs, milk, salt, pepper, and mustard with a whisk and pour over the cheese and ham. Cover with foil and bake in a 350°F oven for 1 hour. Remove the foil and return to oven for an additional 15 minutes. Serve hot.

You can certainly play around with this casserole: add shredded onion, peppers, cooked bacon or cooked sausage instead of ham; add broccoli, spinach — anything you can imagine! Goes well with toasted everything bagel, biscuits, or especially the savoury cheesy biscuits we've made on the show before.

MARY'S SMOKED HADDOCK FISHCAKES
AND GARDEN RELISH

Chef Mary Gillis from Antigonish was on Tunes and Wooden Spoons Facebook *livestream and made these delicious fishcakes along with her signature relish.*

INGREDIENTS

Cold mashed potatoes:
8 large Russet potatoes
1 cup salted butter
4 large tablespoons sour cream
Salt and pepper

Smoked haddock:
1 pound smoked haddock
1 cup salted butter
1 white onion
2 cloves pickled garlic
2 cups white wine
2 pounds fresh haddock fillet
500 ml whipping cream
Fresh green onion
Salt and pepper
Flour for dusting
Butter and vegetable oil for frying cakes

METHOD

Boil potatoes and drain. Leave on warm heat for 5 minutes to evaporate water, then add butter and sour cream and mash. Cool in fridge. (Leftover potatoes are perfect for this.)

Simmer the smoked haddock, onion, garlic and white wine on low heat for 15 minutes or until nice and soft. Add the fresh haddock and cream. Cook for 30 minutes or until well reduced. Add salt and pepper and set aside to cool.

Mix fish and green onion into cold mashed potatoes, and form into cakes. Dust in flour and sauté on medium heat.

Garden-Fresh Cucumber Tomato Balsamic Relish

INGREDIENTS

2 English cucumbers
3 large tomatoes
1 large red onion
Pinch salt
1/2 cup balsamic vinegar
3 tablespoons brown sugar
1 cup vegetable oil
1 lemon
Fresh dill
Salt and pepper

METHOD

Seed and dice cucumber and tomato. Dice red onion. Sprinkle with salt and then drain. Whisk balsamic vinegar, brown sugar, chopped dill, lemon juice and zest with vegetable oil and season with salt and pepper

Featured Grandmother

Sandra Sutherland

"She's just all around fantastic!"

Sandra Sutherland of Port Hood, Nova Scotia, is a grandmother who is cherished beyond measure. A retired school secretary, she now dedicates her time to what she loves most — cooking for her family.

Always found in the kitchen of her beautiful home, Sandra has an endless collection of cookbooks, each one a source of inspiration for the delicious meals she lovingly prepares. An Acadian by birth (a LeBlanc), she grew up enjoying traditional Acadian dishes, but developed a deep appreciation for the rich flavours of the French Canadian Tourtière.

Discovering the recipe in one of her treasured cookbooks, she adapted it to make it her own — a perfect blend of beef and pork wrapped in a golden crust. Though she intended to make just one pie for our visit, she found it nearly impossible, as she is accustomed to baking many at once, especially during Christmas, to share with her family. Served alongside her special stuffing and homemade cranberry sauce, her tourtière was nothing short of spectacular.

Beyond the kitchen, Sandra's creativity shines in other ways. She enjoys crocheting and recently completed a stunning blanket, a testament to her patience and skill. In the summer, her flower gardens are a work of art, admired by many and bursting with colour and life.

The love and care she pours into her cooking, crafting, and gardening are evident in everything she does. Sitting in her warm and welcoming home, it was clear why Sandra is so adored — her home is a place where family, tradition, and love come together in the most beautiful and delicious ways.

FRENCH CANADIAN TOURTIÈRE

Sandra Sutherland's recipe

INGREDIENTS

Pastry:

2 cups flour
1 cup shortening
5 tablespoons cold water

Pie filling:

1 pound lean pork
1 pound lean ground beef
½ cup chopped onions
½ cup chopped celery
½ teaspoon cloves
½ teaspoon nutmeg
½ teaspoon cinnamon
½ teaspoon salt
½ teaspoon pepper
½ teaspoon minced garlic
1 ½ cups beef broth

METHOD

Mix the flour and shortening until mealy and sprinkle with cold water and bring it together with a fork until dough comes together. Try not to overhandle it. Cut dough in half and roll out each half.

Cook the meats with onions and celery and spices until browned. Add the beef broth and simmer for approximately 20 minutes. Cool to room temperature.

Place one rolled crust into a deep-dish 8-inch pie plate and spoon cooled meat mixture into the pie shell. Place the top crust on, trim, and seal well by crimping the edges. Bake in a 400°F oven for 35 minutes or until nicely browned. Best served with gravy and a scoop of dressing.

Sandra's advice to her grandchildren:
"The days are long, but the years are short. Life is busy but make it a priority to call or check in with your parents and grandparents on a regular basis. They love to hear from you."

CHICKEN POT PIE

An easy lunch or supper – we have it often.

INGREDIENTS

1 full pie crust to fit 9-inch pie plate (see pie crust recipe on following page)
2 medium potatoes, diced
1 large carrot, diced
½ cup butter
1 small onion, chopped fine
½ cup flour
1 teaspoon salt
½ teaspoon thyme
½ teaspoon poultry seasoning
½ teaspoon pepper
1 ½ cups chicken broth
¾ cup milk
2 cups cooked cubed chicken
½ cup frozen peas
½ cup frozen corn

METHOD

Boil potatoes and carrots until almost done (bring to a boil and simmer for about 8-10 minutes). Drain and set aside.

In a large pot, melt the butter and add the onion and sauté for about 2 minutes. You're making a roux so stir in the flour and seasonings and whisk well. Gradually pour in the broth and milk and whisk quickly until all is incorporated. Stir in chicken and all veggies. Remove from heat.

Pour the chicken mixture into the prepared pie crust and cover with the second crust. Using scissors, cut around the pie crust, leaving a 1-inch overhang. Now fold that overhang under all the way around and then pinch the edges together, sealing the pie crust. Cut the top with a sharp knife to let steam out.

Bake at 425°F for 40 minutes or more. Let stand for 15 minutes before cutting and serving.

OR spoon the chicken mixture into a 9x13-pan and dollop with biscuit dough and spread out over top. The chicken mixture is already cooked, so bake until biscuit topping is cooked (probably about 18 minutes). When serving, just scoop out – messy, but still delicious!

This dish freezes well. When removing from freezer, let stand at room temperature for about 30 minutes only. Preheat oven to 425°F and bake for 30 minutes. Reduce heat to 350°F and bake a further 70 minutes or so.

Pie Crust

INGREDIENTS

2 cups flour
1 teaspoon salt
⅔ cup shortening

METHOD

Mix all ingredients well until crumbly and add 5 tablespoons ice-cold water. Mix with a fork until the pastry comes together. With your hands, gather the dough into a ball and sprinkle the ball with flour until not sticky. Divide in two and roll out each dough ball to about 12 inches and place the crust in an un-greased 9-inch pie plate.

Featured Grandmother

Mary Dickinson
"Grammy's food is amazing."

Mary's advice to her grandchildren:
"Be kind to one another."

GRAMMY D'S MAC AND CHEESE

Mary Dickinson's recipe.

INGREDIENTS

2 cups dry macaroni

Sauce:

3 tablespoons butter
3 tablespoons flour
3 cups milk (or upscale to 18% half-and-half/coffee cream)
8-10 ounces grated old cheddar cheese (about 3 cups)
½ teaspoon grated onion
½-1 teaspoon Worcestershire sauce
1 teaspoon prepared mustard
½ teaspoon salt
Shake of pepper

Topping:

2-3 ounces grated mozzarella cheese (about ⅓ cup)
¾ cup seasoned breadcrumbs mixed with 1 tablespoon melted butter

METHOD

Butter a 2-quart casserole dish and preheat oven to 350°F.

Cook macaroni in 6-8 cups boiling, salted water for 7-8 minutes only, then drain.

While the macaroni is cooking, make the sauce. Using a microwavable 8 cup bowl, melt the butter and add the onion and flour and stir until smooth. Place in microwave on medium-high for approximately 30 seconds. Stir. Add the milk (or cream) a little at a time and stir until smooth. Microwave on high for approximately 1 minute, stir, and then return to microwave for another minute until slightly thickened.

Add the mustard, Worcestershire sauce, salt, and pepper. Stir and add the grated cheese (about a cup at a time), and after each addition, microwave on medium-high for about a minute until cheese is melted. Stir as you go.

Mix the sauce with the drained macaroni. Pour into casserole dish. Sprinkle with grated mozzarella cheese and then sprinkle with the buttered breadcrumbs.

Bake until cheese is melted and the casserole is hot and bubbly (about 15-20 minutes). For a golden-brown top, switch the oven to broil for the last couple of minutes.

Yield: 4-6 servings

From the moment we stepped into Mary Dickinson's home in Fredericton, New Brunswick, we were wrapped in warmth and kindness. Dressed in a black sweater to match mine, accessorized with dangly earrings and red lipstick, we were like twins at first sight!

Mary's husband, Dalton, greeted us with a warm welcome before leaving us ladies to our morning of baking, cooking, tea, and heartfelt conversation. Joining us were Mary and Dalton's daughter-in-law Cheyenne and their three granddaughters — Molly, Emmie, and Sadie — who had proudly nominated their beloved Grammy for this book.

Mary and Dalton have three children and nine grandchildren, and they all feel the same about this wonderful Grammy and her love of sharing goodies and meals with them. They say she is the glue that keeps everyone connected and it's not unusual to find her and Dalton dropping off treats or a small meal at their doorsteps on holidays or special life events, when they can't all gather together.

Mary had a beautiful spread waiting for us, featuring her famous "Grammy D's Mac and Cheese," her delicate shortbread cookies, and her signature "Kindness Cake," a recipe you'll find on page 77. As we enjoyed every delicious bite, two of Mary's dearest friends, Sheila and Paula, dropped in, adding even more warmth and laughter to an already special visit.

Beyond her talents in the kitchen, Mary is known for something even greater — her unwavering commitment to her community. A tireless volunteer, she steps up wherever there is a need, with a special place in her heart for working with refugees. If help is required, Mary is there — every single time. Meeting her, her family, and her friends was a true gift, and if I lived closer, I know she would be one of my best friends. She is deeply loved by her children, grandchildren, and all those who are lucky enough to know her.

DIPS, PRESERVES, AND SIDES

NANCY'S GREAT GOBS OF GRATITUDE GRANOLA

Author and television personality Nancy Regan was a guest on Tunes and Wooden Spoons *and made this granola – to die for!*

INGREDIENTS

½ cup coconut flakes (unsweetened)
2 cups slivered almonds
1 ½ cups pecans
1 ½ cups walnuts
3 tablespoons (+) chia seeds
3 tablespoons flaxseed meal
1 ½ teaspoons cinnamon (optional)
2-3 cups rolled oats
3 tablespoons coconut sugar
¼ tsp. salt
⅓ cup coconut oil (or butter)
¼ cup maple syrup
Optional: pumpkin seeds, sunflower seeds, hemp hearts, dried cranberries or blueberries, etc.

METHOD

Set oven to 325°F. Mix all ingredients together and bake on cookies sheets for about 20 minutes until crispy, stirring every 5-6 minutes.

Nancy says, "Make adjustments as you like to suit your personal taste."

Enjoy!

CRANBERRY PECAN CHUTNEY

Mary Frances Leahy – daughter of Natalie MacMaster and Donnell Leahy, fiddler — is a piano player, step-dancer, singer, and more. She was a guest on Tunes and Wooden Spoons *and made this delicious chutney that is a staple at gatherings in the Leahy household.*

INGREDIENTS

- ¼ cup plus 2 teaspoons butter, divided
- 1 cup finely diced red onion (about ½ onion)
- ½ cup Thompson raisins
- 1 tablespoon dark rum
- ½ cup water
- ½ cup dried cranberries
- ½ cup finely chopped pecan halves
- ⅓ cup firmly packed brown sugar
- 2 teaspoons vanilla

METHOD

Heat 2 teaspoons butter in a large skillet. Sauté onions and raisins in the butter for about 4 minutes. Add the rum and stir over medium heat.

When rum evaporates (about 2 minutes), add the water and continue cooking until liquid is absorbed (about another 2 minutes). Add the ¼ cup butter, pecans, cranberries, and brown sugar and sauté for about 1 minute. Add vanilla and cook for 5 minutes over medium heat, stirring frequently.

Serve over a toasted baguette (slice the baguette diagonally into ¾ inch slices, place on a parchment-lined baking sheet, brush with olive oil, and place in a 350°F oven for 15 minutes). Remove and add 2-3 slices of cheese of your choice (a 3-5 year aged cheddar is nice) and top with the warm chutney; serve up immediately! So good – sweet and savoury all together!

JORDAN'S BACON JAM

My neighbour Jordan van den Heuvel dropped in at Christmas and gave us a small bottle of his bacon jam. It was a big hit, and he was hounded for the recipe which he didn't have because he just threw it together and didn't have amounts. So, he set about re-creating it and followed through with the following ingredients and method. It's a winner!

INGREDIENTS

1 pound bacon (diced in 1-inch pieces)
1 medium onion, diced
3 cloves garlic, minced
½ cup brown sugar
½ cup apple cider vinegar
½ cup maple syrup
1 tablespoon hot sauce
1 jalapeño pepper, diced (optional)

METHOD

Fry the bacon. Remove the bacon and in the grease add the diced onion and garlic and sauté until softened. Add the sugar, vinegar, maple syrup, and hot sauce and stir on medium-high for 10-15 minutes. Add the chopped bacon and stir until it begins to thicken. Jar the jam.

Serve on scallops, hamburgers, pork chops, cheese and crackers, atop Brie (or other) cheese, and also on Oliver's Patty Melts (recipe on page 167).

HOT CHICKEN DIP

When Roots 223 were entertaining on the Tunes and Wooden Spoons *show, this is the dip that was shared by the group. Truly addictive!*

INGREDIENTS

1 pound of chicken breast, cooked and shredded (about 3 medium-sized chicken breasts)
8 ounces softened cream cheese (1 brick)
1 cup blue cheese dressing
½ cup Dave's hot sauce
1 cup shredded cheddar cheese

METHOD

Mix together and place in baking dish (similar to the size of an 8x8-inch pan). Top with another ½ cup of shredded cheese.

Bake 15-20 minutes at 350°F until cheese bubbles. Use nachos, baguettes, crackers for scooping.

Homemade Blue Cheese Dressing

INGREDIENTS

⅓ cup sour cream
⅓ cup mayo
3 ounces crumbled blue cheese
1 tablespoon or more of minced parsley
1 tablespoon lemon juice
Salt and pepper

METHOD

Mix well. Great as a dip, but if you want to have as a salad dressing, just add a little milk until you get the right consistency. So delicious.

LOBSTER DIP

I am not a lobster lover – but this dip recipe, shared by Debbie MacDonald, is well-loved when I make and share it with friends.

INGREDIENTS

1 package cream cheese, softened
1 cup mayo
1 cup grated aged cheddar
2 cups cooked diced lobster
(approximately 2 lobsters)
1 tablespoon dried dill
2 tablespoons minced onion
Salt and pepper to taste

METHOD

Mix all together and place in a lightly buttered casserole dish. Bake in a 320°F oven until heated through (about 20 minutes). Serve warm with crackers or pita bites.

UGLY DIP

A dip from daughter-in-law Kelli; she doesn't recall why it's called Ugly Dip, but it tastes amazing!

INGREDIENTS

1 cup finely chopped pecans
1 cup of chopped green onion
2 cups shredded cheese
Half a small jar of hot pepper jelly

METHOD

Mix all together and serve with nachos, beet chips, or crackers.

MAMA'S MINCEMEAT

This is the mincemeat recipe that I grew up on. It is certainly delicious in pie and tarts, but I used to have it warmed in a bowl and would have it for breakfast with a biscuit. Mama would say, "Eat it, it is full of iron." And so I did.

INGREDIENTS

3 pounds roast beef
½ pound suet
10 medium apples
3 cups molasses
2 lemons (pulp only, no rind)
2 pounds (907 grams) sticky raisins (Lexia raisins)
2 pounds (907 grams) currants
1 pound (453 grams) sultana raisins
2 teaspoons nutmeg
2 teaspoons cloves
3 tablespoons cinnamon
1 tablespoon salt
2.2 pounds/1 kg brown sugar
2 cups orange juice
1 cup water
½ cup vinegar
½ cup grapefruit juice
2 tablespoons vanilla

METHOD

Cut up the roast beef into about 3-inch (7.5cm) cubes and place in Dutch oven. Cover with water. Bring to a boil and simmer until tender (maybe an hour). Put through grinder along with the suet (available from your butcher).

Peel and slice apples and cook until slightly tender. Drain water and mash apples. Combine other ingredients and place in a large pot and simmer for 1 ½ hours.

Place in a crock and store in a cold room. Or you can bottle and seal while hot and suet will raise to the top. Store in fridge or freezer – don't fill too full.

Featured Grandmother

Margaret (Margie) MacInnis

"When anyone stayed the night, they'd wake up to a big scoff in the morning."

MANDARIN MACARONI SALAD

Margie MacInnis' recipe

INGREDIENTS

1 cup mayonnaise
2 tablespoons milk
2 tablespoons lemon juice
1 tablespoon white sugar
½ teaspoon salt
1 ½ cups cooked macaroni
1 can mandarin oranges, drained
1 chopped apple
1 cup diced celery

METHOD

Stir together the mayonnaise, milk, lemon juice, sugar, and salt.

Add remaining ingredients. Toss and cover well and refrigerate.

One of the most beautiful souls I've ever had the privilege of meeting is Margie MacInnis of West Mabou, Nova Scotia. Originally from Judique, she may have changed her address, but the warm coastal air of West Mabou seems to suit her just fine.

Margie lost her beloved husband, Jimmy, more than a decade ago, but their son, Peter, and his wife, Lisa, have blessed her with three wonderful grandchildren who fill her days with love, laughter, and purpose. Jimmy would have been an incredible grandfather, but life has its own timing.

Margie has always been the life of the party — the ultimate hostess to the countless people who have passed through her home and legendary garage gatherings, filled with fiddles, laughter, and dancing that lasted well into the night. She and Jimmy were the heart and soul behind the weekly square dances in West Mabou, keeping the tradition alive through rain, snow, and sleet. Thanks to their dedication, dancers from near and far were given a stage to experience the magic of a Cape Breton square dance.

Beyond the dance hall, Margie is a pillar of her community. She never hesitates to bring a meal to someone living alone, and she's always lending a hand — whether it's stitching a hem, whipping up a batch of something delicious, or helping Peter with the children and farm chores. She's a familiar sight at every parade in Mabou, Port Hood, and Judique, dressed to the nines and riding her festively decorated tandem bicycle. She's the first to play a good-natured prank and is the keeper of family history, penning heartfelt poems for special occasions that capture the essence of love and tradition.

Her son, Peter, reflects on their home growing up: "Our doors were never locked — people were always coming and going, and our home was filled with food, music, stories, and laughter. After the dances, my father would invite a crowd up, leaving my mother to pull together tea and a feast in no time. And in the morning, guests woke up to a big scoff, leaving with full bellies and full hearts. That's just who she is."

Margie MacInnis embodies the spirit of Cape Breton hospitality, and if ever there were a statue erected at the Canso Causeway in her honour, the plaque would surely read: "The Queen of Cape Breton Hospitality."

Margie's advice to her grandchildren: *"What a mercy there is no tax on grandchildren, sunshine, and humour!"*

MJ'S TURKEY STUFFING

This is how I made my turkey stuffing – increase the spices if you like a stronger flavour.

INGREDIENTS

10 slices white bread (about 8 cups of fresh bread when ripped into pieces for toasting, and yields a little more than 2 cups of crumbs when crushed after toasting)
7 medium potatoes
¾ cup butter
3 teaspoons poultry seasoning
3 teaspoons sage
2 teaspoons summer savoury
2 teaspoons salt
1 ½ teaspoons pepper
1 teaspoon white sugar
1 small onion (grated) OR 2 teaspoons onion powder

METHOD

Rip the bread into smaller pieces and place on a large baking sheet in a 325°F oven for about 20-25 minutes. At the half-way mark, stir up the bread pieces. Remove from oven and set aside for about 20 minutes.

Meanwhile, peel potatoes, wash, cut into smaller pieces, and place in a pot and cover with water. Bring to a boil and cook until tender. Drain and mash without adding anything. Set aside.

Once the bread pieces are cooled, leave them on the baking sheet and take a rolling pin and crush the bread until it is the consistency of fine crumbs.

In a large saucepan, melt the butter over low heat and add the grated onion and stir for 1 minute. If not using grated onion, add the onion powder and all other seasonings and stir until combined with the melted butter. Remove from heat. Add the breadcrumbs and make sure all is combined. Add mashed potatoes and using a potato masher, combine all ingredients together until completely incorporated. Do a taste test – if you like it, great; if you want more spice, add more salt and a bit more of the sage, savoury, or poultry seasonings to taste (1/2 teaspoon at best of each).

The stuffing should stick together at this point when you test a bit in your fist. If stuffing a turkey, the best way is to measure a large piece of cheesecloth and place the stuffing on top and then bring together into a 'bag' and stuff the bag into the turkey with open end out. Tie the loose ends with string. Place the turkey into the oven to bake and when done, it is easy to pull the bag out and place the stuffing in a bowl for serving.

CINNAMON DRESSING

Jessie MacDonald's grandmother was born in 1887. From at least that time, if not generations before, this recipe has been passed down through the ages and today Jessie does not have a family gathering without this very special dressing.

INGREDIENTS

5 pounds potatoes, cooked and mashed
1 cup melted butter
1 medium onion diced
¼ cup white sugar
4 teaspoons cinnamon
8 slices day-old bread ripped in pieces
4 teaspoons salt

METHOD

Mash the potatoes and add the diced bread, onion, melted butter, and mix together. Add the salt, sugar, cinnamon, and salt together and sprinkle over the potato mixture. Mix well with your hands until mixture comes together.

Jessie forms four rectangular "loaves," wraps each of them in foil, and places them on a cookie sheet. Bake at 350°F for 1 hour in total. At the 45-minute mark of baking, open up the foil to expose the loaf and continue baking for an additional 15 minutes, or until the dressing gets a little crispy brown on the edges. Serve warm and slice or scoop up with your favourite dinner.

PUP'S ZUCCHINI RELISH

Shared by Herb Bonvic, an avid cook and our son's neigbour.

INGREDIENTS

12 cups unpeeled zucchini
4 large onions
2 red peppers
2 green peppers
½ cup pickling salt
3 cups white vinegar
2 teaspoons celery seed
2 teaspoons turmeric
2 teaspoons mustard seed
4 cups white sugar
3 tablespoons cornstarch
2 tablespoons water

METHOD

Dice the vegetables very small (relish size) or use a food processor to chop into pieces.

Combine the vegetables and sprinkle the salt over the mixture. Cover and set aside overnight (or about 8 hours). Drain and rinse with cold water.

Place the vegetables in a large pot and add the vinegar, celery seed, turmeric, mustard seed, and sugar. Mix well and bring to a simmer.

Make a slurry with the cornstarch and water and add to the vegetable mixture. Stir until it thickens and continue simmering for 2-3 minutes. Bottle in sterile jars.

COWBOY CANDY

If you want a hit of heat on burgers or nachos, this is the real deal!

INGREDIENTS

1 ½ pounds fresh jalapeños (about 30 peppers)
1 cup apple cider vinegar
3 cups white sugar
1 teaspoon garlic powder
¼ teaspoon ground turmeric
¼ teaspoon celery seed

METHOD

Remove the stems from the peppers and discard. Slice the peppers into ¼-inch slices. Set aside. In a Dutch oven pot, add the vinegar, white sugar, garlic powder, turmeric, and celery seed and bring to a boil. Reduce the heat and simmer for 5 minutes. Turn the heat to medium-high and bring to a boil again. Once boiling, add the peppers and return to a boil. Reduce the heat and simmer for about 4 minutes.

Using a slotted spoon, transfer the pepper mixture to sterile jars, filling to within ¼ inch of the rim. With the remaining syrup, bring to a full rolling boil and let boil for about 6 minutes. Ladle the syrup into the jars to a quarter of an inch from the rim.

LORRAINE LANE SALSA

Lorraine Lane is the street where our son Mitchell and his wife Laura live. This community of friends and neighbours is the absolute best. The Lorraine Lane Salsa recipe is often shared on the street. Thanks to Gerarda Bonvie for sharing it with me!

INGREDIENTS

8 cups tomatoes, chopped
2 ½ cups onions, chopped
1 ½ cups green pepper, chopped
2 jalapeño peppers, seeded and chopped
6 cloves garlic, minced
2 teaspoons cumin
2 tablespoons salt
1 cup vinegar
⅛ cup parsley
2 teaspoons pepper
⅓ cup sugar
2-16 ounce cans tomato paste

METHOD

Mix all ingredients in a stock pot. Cook mixture on medium-high heat until vegetables are cooked through. Blend with immersion blender. Bring to a boil. Let simmer for 15 minutes. Bottle in sterile jars.

The Kitchen Table

by Margie MacDonald

I've been with her through the years.
Her tears have hit me countless times.

I'm scratched from when she used me as a cutting board.
And oh but the cups of tea!
They have left their marks, but I don't mind.
The world's problems have been solved here around me.
If only they put grandmothers in charge.

I can tell you that no one leaves this table hungry.
And the belly laughs!
As plentiful as the crumbs around my feet.
I've watched her unshakable love for her children.
They have grown into adults
Who often think they know better.

She lets them. But she knows best.
Then came the grandchildren.
She is in her element now.
She tends to them.
Guides them. Feeds them.
Softly scolds them (then gives them a cookie).
She lets them stir the pot.
And break the eggs.
They have the power to break her heart.

But they won't.

They know they can ask her for anything.
As they grow they understand her love's value.
She cooks their favourite meals.
Sends them money when she can.
She marvels at how quickly they've grown.
A sacred patchwork of their smiling faces covers
The fridge across from me.

She has known loss but keeps going.
I hear her say, "What choice is there?"
She chooses love.

Every. Single. Time.

Her quiet strength,
A force that binds the family together.
She sits with me in the morning,
Weathered hands clasped.
She goes through her list of loved ones.
Prays they are safe on the roads. Prays they are all ok.
That their futures are bright and their hearts are happy.

This unbounded love fills every crevice of this home.
I'm sure it flies out the windows
And wraps itself around each and every one of them.

She worries about time slipping away.
Knows tomorrow is not promised.
I'm happy to sit with her on those days.
Her head in her hands.
Her elbows resting on my worn top.
I wish I could tell her she is a gift.
If only she knew the power of her light,
She might see herself the way the world does.
I wish they would tell her more often that she is loved.

The window light drapes softly across her face.
Tracing the lines etched in her skin.
I remember the troubled nights.
The early mornings. The mess.
The gatherings. The stories.
The heartaches and the heart-leaps.
Days spent with worry.
Days spent with sunshine.
Days spent chasing sleep and joy.

Her lines are like my own.
A testimony of life well lived.
She is the kind of beauty you feel
Before you fully understand.
She is a God-given masterpiece.

A knock at the door. She gets up as it opens.
Her shoulders ease. Her heart soars.
Her arms reach out. They've arrived.
Another helping of love soon to be devoured around me.

I've got the best seat in the house.

ACKNOWLEDGEMENTS

To Our Supporters

To MacIntyre Purcell Publishing, especially Jeff Cox, Vernon Oickle, and the whole creative team. Thank you for believing in this book and helping bring it to life so beautifully, and for their belief that we could do "one more book." Thank you so much. We did it!

Destination Cape Breton celebrates the island where we live and their support for this book helped make it happen. Thank you so very much.

Thank you to all those who nominated grandparents and how I wish we could have included everyone.

A special appreciation to the 39 grandmothers and two grandfathers I had the pleasure of visiting. Your stories, love, and food filled both my heart and belly. I will never forget you.

With Special Thanks

Carrie Beaton, cousin and decorator, for always being there when I need you, and big thanks to Maple and Jack Florists, Port Hawkesbury, for the front door arrangement.

Terry MacDonald, artist, for making my grandmothers smile for the first time in their wedding pictures.

Bob Martin Photography for always helping and for always coming through at the last minute.

For all the musicians and creative guests who shared their talents during the 200 shows of *Tunes and Wooden Spoons* – amazing!

For the ladies of Lorraine Lane, Lower South River, for aiding me in my hour of need.

For those who shared recipes with me, there wouldn't be a book without you.

To My Family

My husband, Cecil, – thanks for being my recipe dictation partner, my patient taste-tester (maybe too much), and my steady support through it all. I love you.

With so much love to my children, Tammy, Brennan, Margie, Gordie, Kelly, Krista, and Mitchell. Thank you for always being there when I need you. I love you so very much.

Margie – what a joy to share yet another cookbook with you. Thank you for your beautiful photography, your patience when I stressed over deadlines, and for always saying yes.

Margie asked me to thank Ryan for putting up with her many cookbook road trips with me, her most favourite being the one where she and I were visiting the Port Hood grandmothers. When we got back to home, Ryan was there waiting for her, took her to see the awesome Port Hood sunset, and asked her to marry him. The perfect ending to a perfect day.

Charlie, Oliver, Asher, Ben, Rosie, Luke, Mary Sarah, Iver, Brody, Aiden, Jake, and Anna. I love being your grandmother and appreciate your love for my cooking. On many occasions, when my grandchildren come for a visit, they sometimes will call ahead and request for certain things to be baked and I am so happy to oblige. So for this cookbook, it was my turn and I asked them each to cook or bake something they like and to take a selfie and send it back to me for the cookbook. They didn't hesitate for one minute and it was such a proud moment for me. I appreciate that so much! This is what makes being a grandmother so very special. It's the moments where we get to receive the love and give the love to each and every one of them and I know all the grandmothers (and grandfathers) in this book feel the same way.

Charlie

Oliver

Asher

Ben

Rosie

Luke

Mary Sarah

Iver

Brody

Aiden

Jake

Anna

INDEX

RECIPES

COOKIES and SQUARES

DESSERTS and CAKES

BREADS, MUFFINS, and MORE

SOUPS, CHOWDERS, and QUICK MEALS

DIPS, PRESERVES, and SIDES

FEATURED GRANDMOTHERS AND GRANDFATHERS

OUTTAKES

Left to right: **Rita Landry, Sharon Tayes, George Muise, Heather Connell, Pauline Chisholm, Sharon Roach, Maureen Sutherland, Benjamina MacIsaac,** and **Minnie van de Wiel.**

Left to right: **Donna MacIver**, **Sharon MacGillivray**, **Margie MacInnis**, **Gloria Walsh**, **Gayle MacDonald**, **Anne Boudreau**, **Gloria Smith**, **Julie Devoe**, and **Mary Dickinson**.

LOVE
ONE
ANOTHER